ABANDONED NEW SOUTH WALES

FROM THE BACK OF BOURKE TO BALMAIN AND BEYOND

SHANE THOMS

AUSTRALIA
THROUGH TIME

The creators of this book's content fully acknowledge and recognise the Traditional Custodians of the land on which these structures were built and pay our respects to all elders past, present, and emerging. Although this publication does not deeply explore the Indigenous stories of the spaces explored, the creators of its content recognise that Australia's First Nations people have occupied and cared for this continent for over 65,000 years. And no matter where we are across this nation, Australia always was and always will be Aboriginal and Torres Strait Islander land.

Australia Through Time
is an imprint jointly owned by

Woodslane Press Pty Ltd, 10 Apollo Street, Warriewood, NSW 2102, Australia
Email: info@woodslane.com.au
Tel: 02 8445 2300
Website: www.woodslanepress.com.au

and

Fonthill Media, Millview, Toadsmoor Road, Stroud, GL5 2TB, United Kingdom
Tel: 01453 886959
Website: www.fonthill.media

First published in Australia in 2023 by Fonthill Media and Woodslane Press

NATIONAL LIBRARY OF AUSTRALIA
A catalogue record for this book is available from the National Library of Australia

MIX
Paper from responsible sources
FSC www.fsc.org FSC® C151165

Printed in China by Jilin GIGO

WOODSLANE PRESS

FONTHILL

CONTENTS

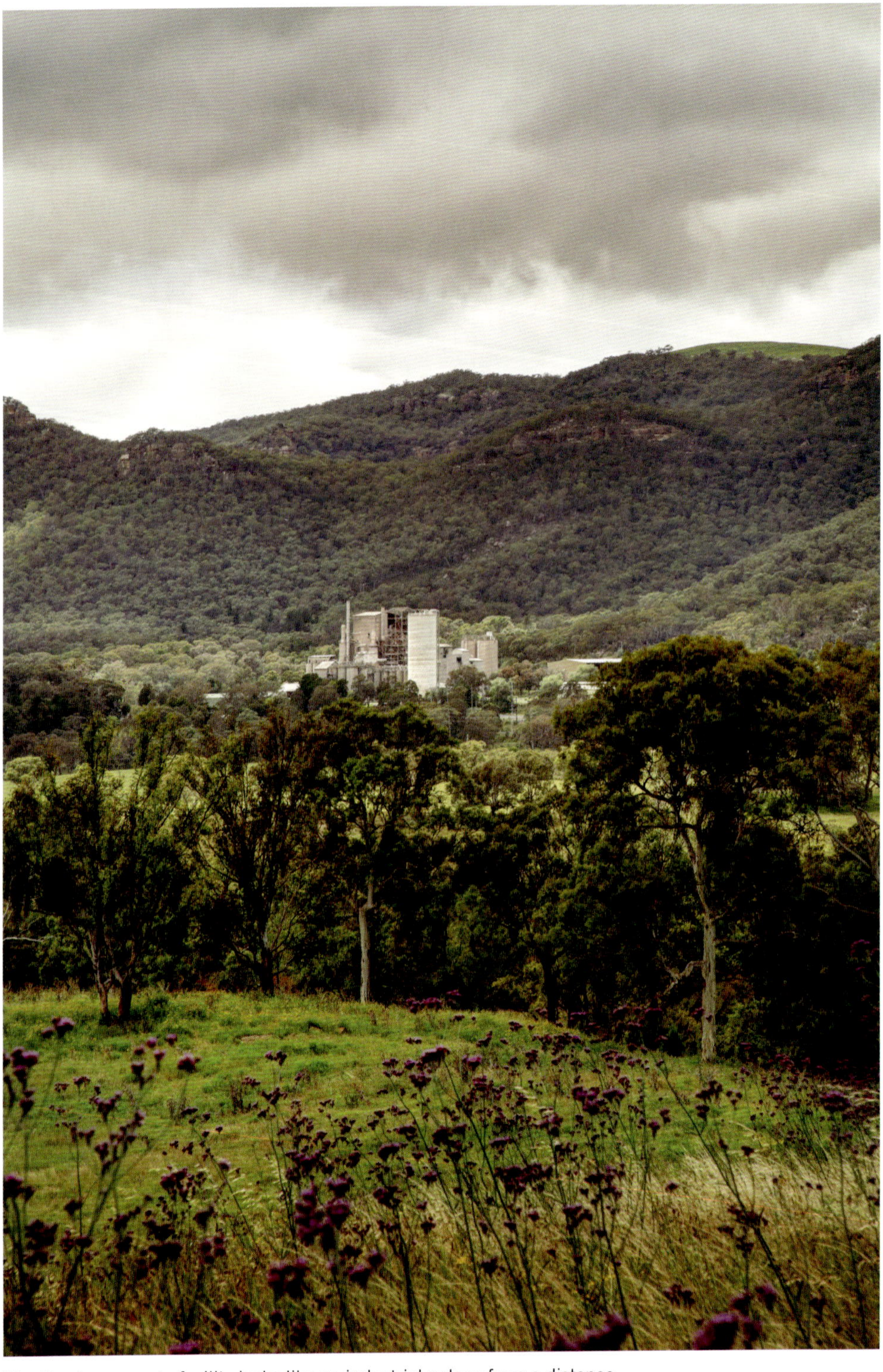

The Kandos concrete facility looks like an industrial palace from a distance

INTRODUCTION

ABANDONED NEW SOUTH WALES

From the Opera House, sitting like a jewel embedded in the Sydney crown, to the warm northern beaches and, much farther west, to the sprawling red deserts surrounding Broken Hill, New South Wales is diverse and bountiful.

The region is the traditional realm of many Indigenous groups, dating back over 60,000 years, from the Gadigal people in Sydney to the Bundjalung, Ngarabal and Kamilaroi people in the north, the central Wiradjuri people, the Yuin and Ngarigo people in the South and the Paakantyi people to the West. Their footprints, ancient and new, will always be embedded in the soil of this sun-baked land.

Colonised in 1788 as a British penal outpost, the majority of the state's Eastern coastal regions were utilised for farming and agriculture. However, a timeline crammed with industry offshoring, changes in consumer demand, and ongoing variances in social demographics has left a trail of architectural legacies in its wake. Each with a unique story, the abandoned factories, homes, convents, churches or any one of these discarded establishments are the small footnotes left by the most recent occupants of these spaces. By closely examining them, we're granted an opportunity to reconstruct each story and, permitting enough props have been left behind, to guess at the narratives that once played out on each stage.

It is here that the past and present clash together to reveal a handful of small vignettes that whisper the secrets of those who came to live and dwell. Abandoned New South Wales points to some of the clues that speak of the forgotten lives of Australia's most populous state.

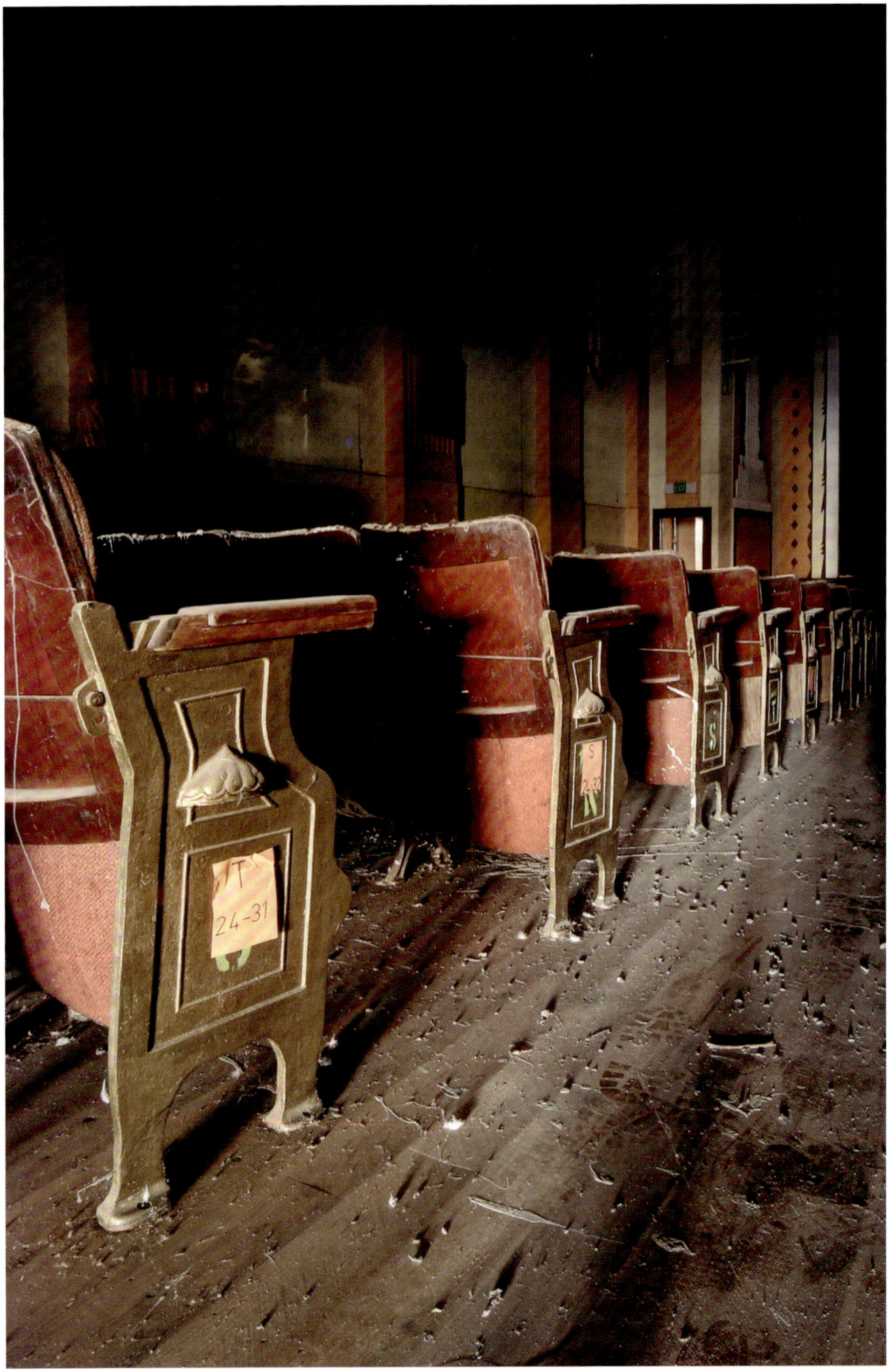

The Regent Theatre's dusty auditorium

THE REGENT THEATRE

Built in 1935, this classic Art Deco relic housed up to 686 patrons in the stalls, with space for an additional 300 on its upper balcony. Designed by a prominent architect, this classic structure was placed on the National Trust Register in September 1993. But in 2009, the cinema rolled down the ticket box shutters and switched off the projectors for the last time.

Located in the Central Western township of Mudgee, the facility acted as an entertainment hub for this tight-knit country community. Supposedly designed and styled to replicate Sydney's very own Regent Theatre, the complex was, at one stage, the largest in Australia and boasted the widest screen.

Embellished with all the trademarks of the Art Deco era, its ornate features and original light fixtures still decorate its walls and high ceilings. Upstairs, the building's tight, attic-like projection room is crammed with vintage items from cinematic days long since passed. Film reels, light bulbs, fuses, switches and operational knick-knacks lay scattered across bench tops and floors while, down below, rows of cracked leather seats line an auditorium now covered in cobwebs.

Standing in the Regent Theatre is a contemplative experience where the narrative has leaped from the screen and the visual drama manifests in the real-time environment. Once providing a window to the outer world throughout the wartime period and beyond, this timeless theatre is a significant structure that not only documents Australia's flirtation with the Art Deco era but houses an abundance of generational memories.

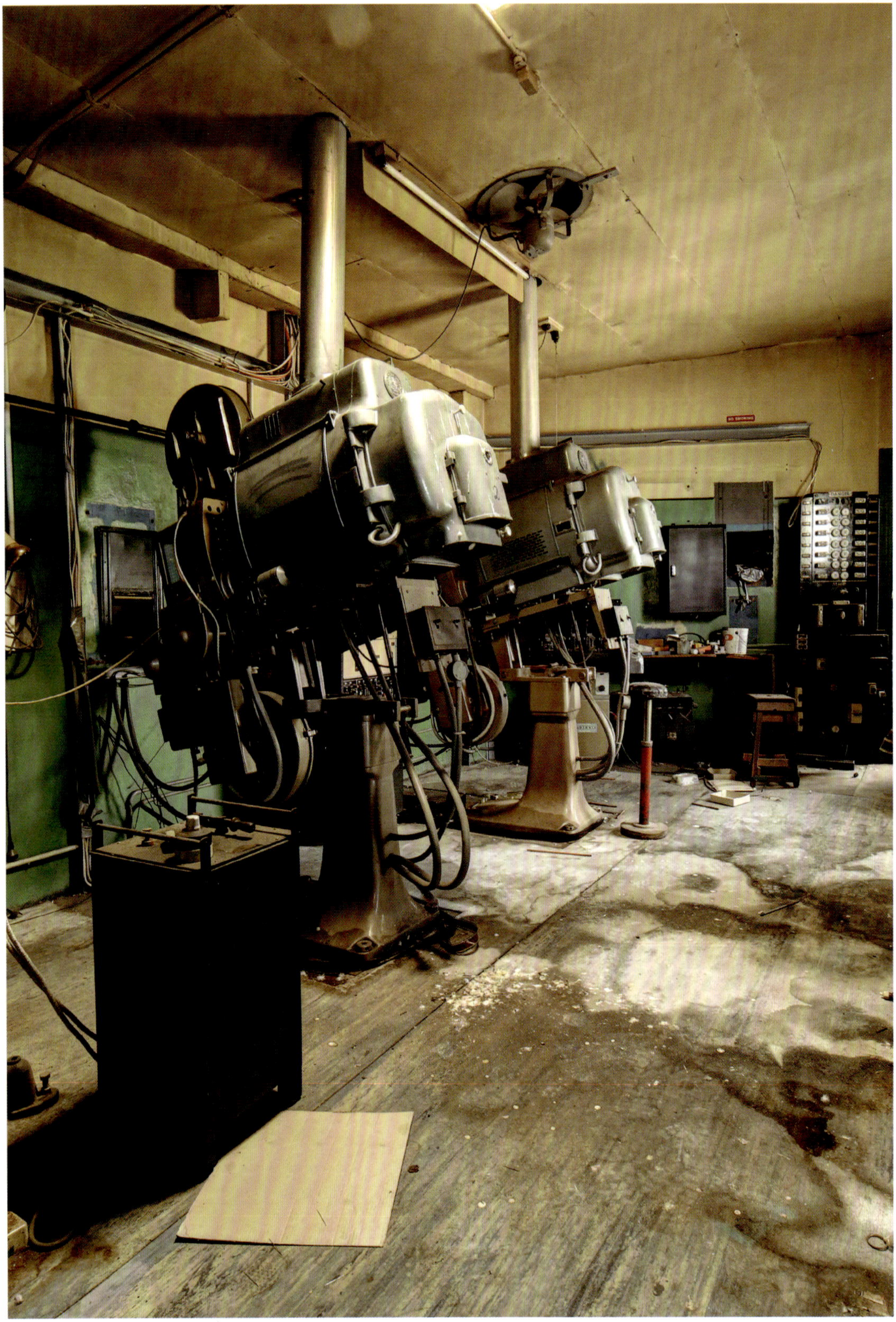

The attic-like former projection room

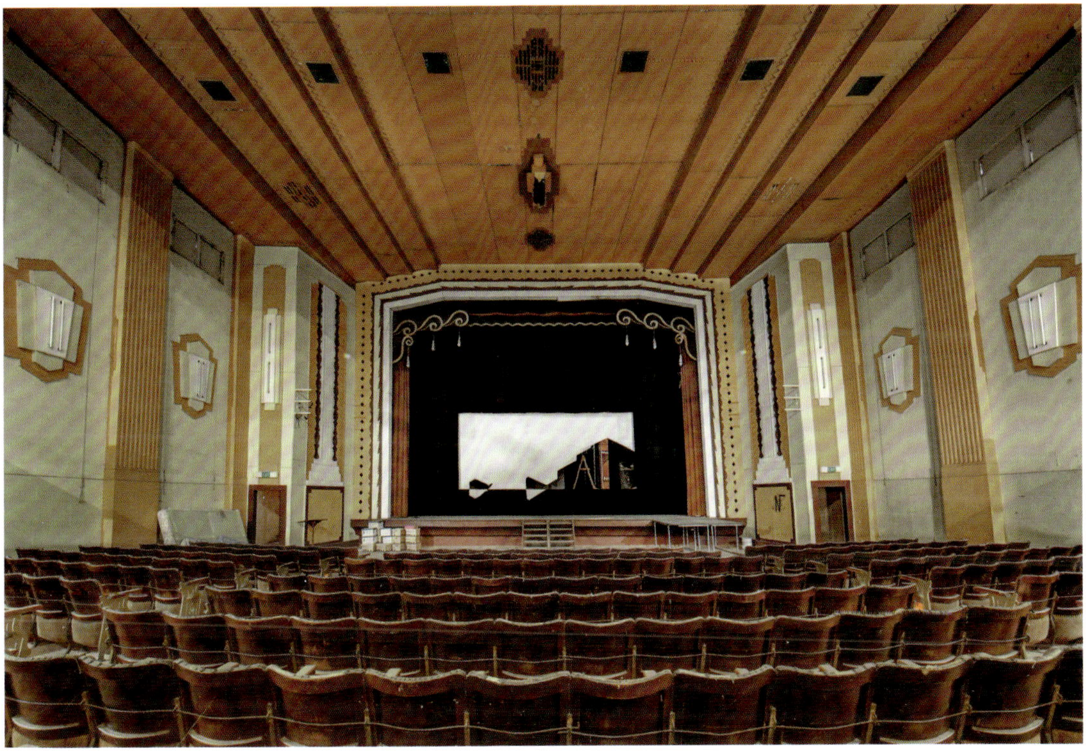
A view of the theatre's large auditorium, lined with original Art Deco features

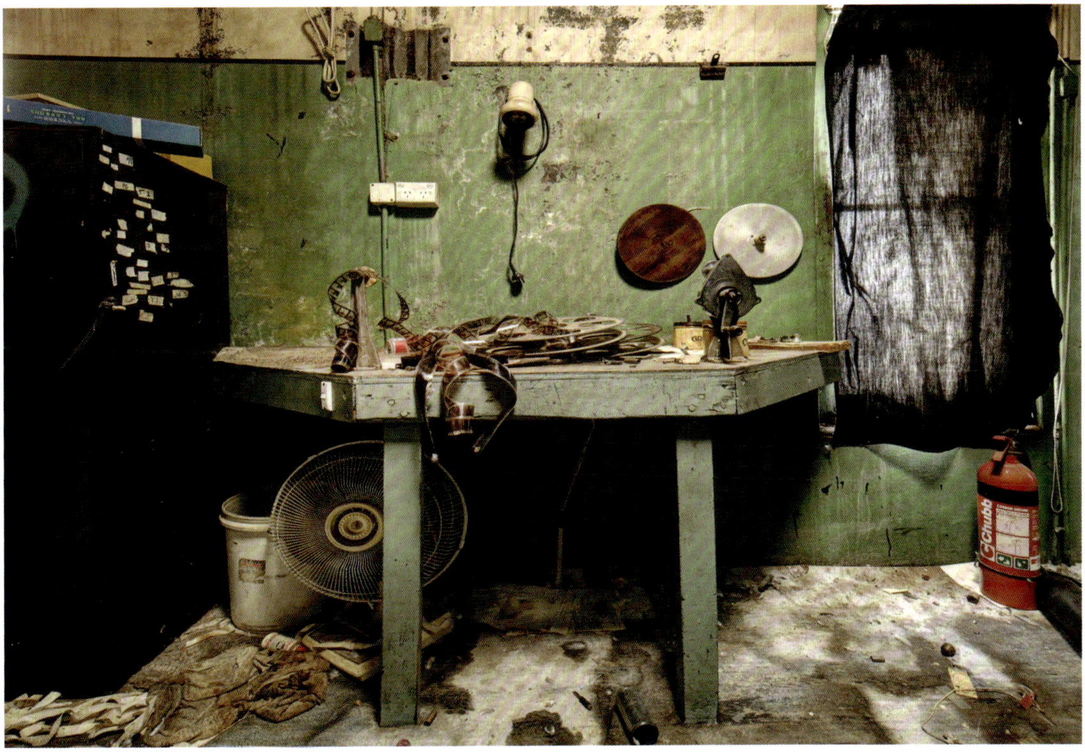
Film reels remain on a worktable in the projection room

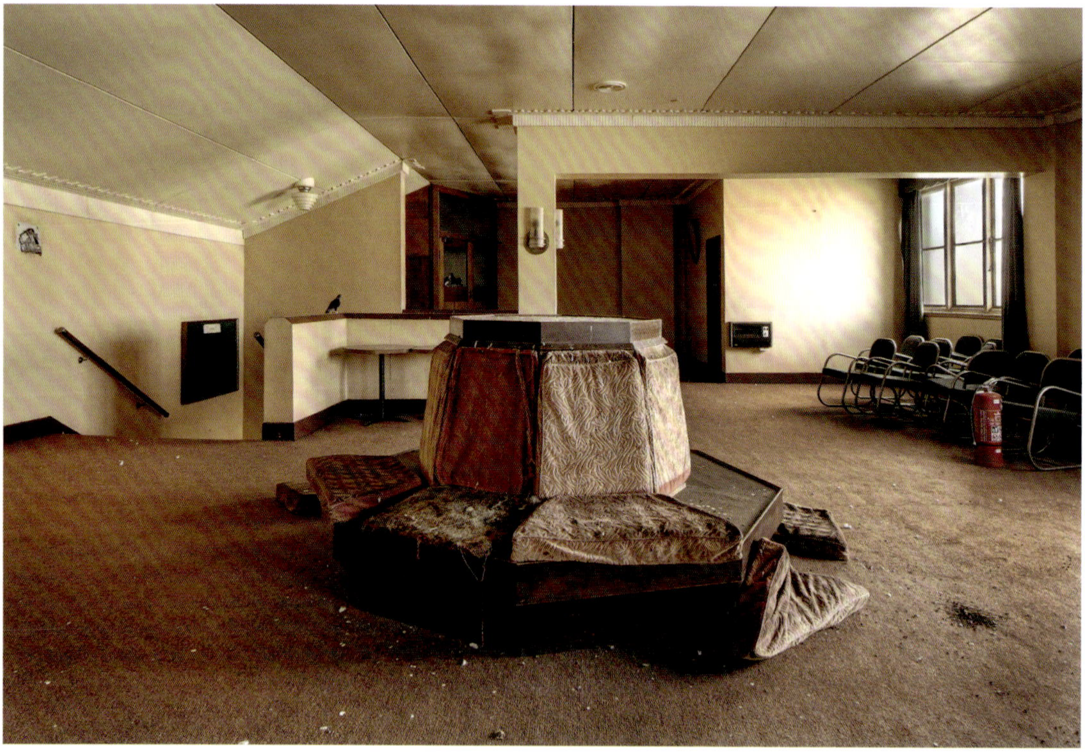

The intermission lounge

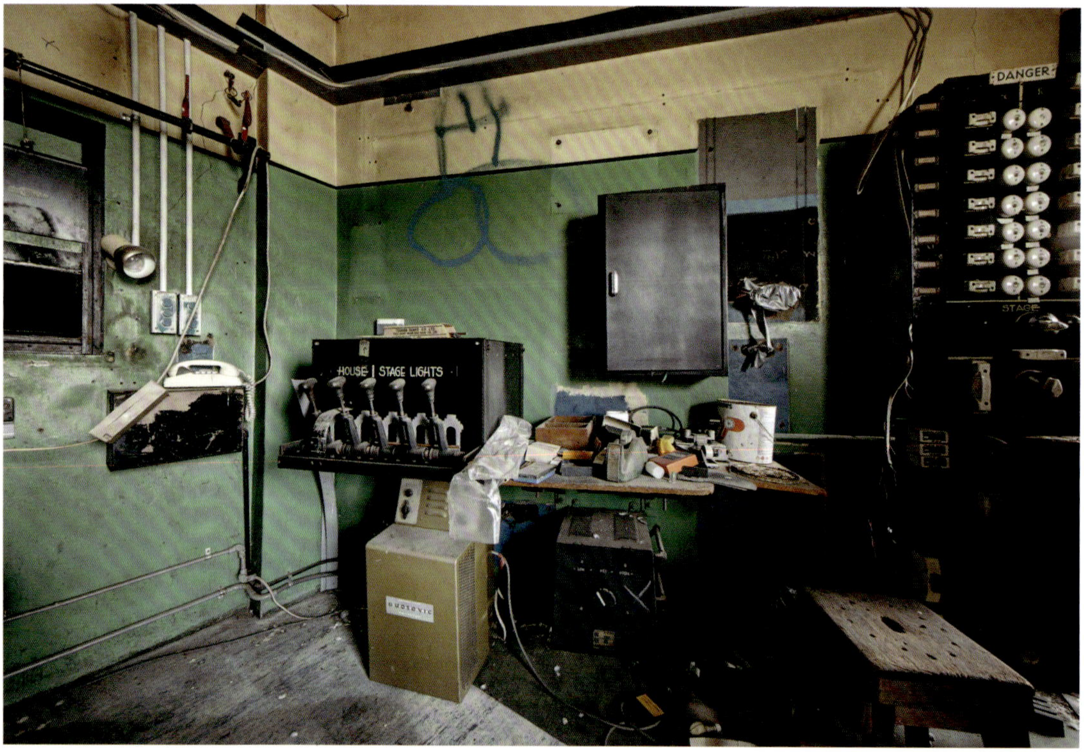

The control panels and lighting switches

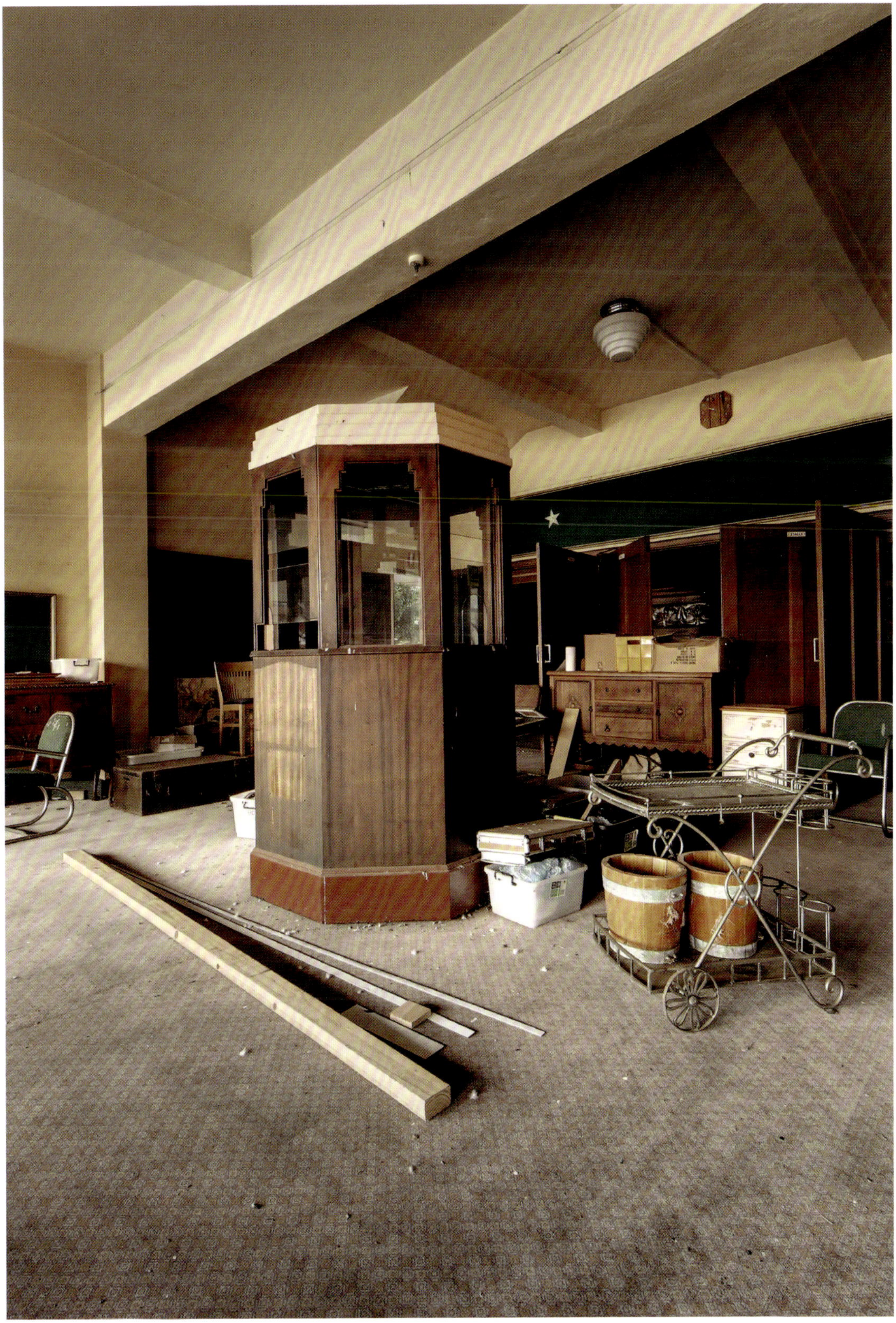

The original ticket box

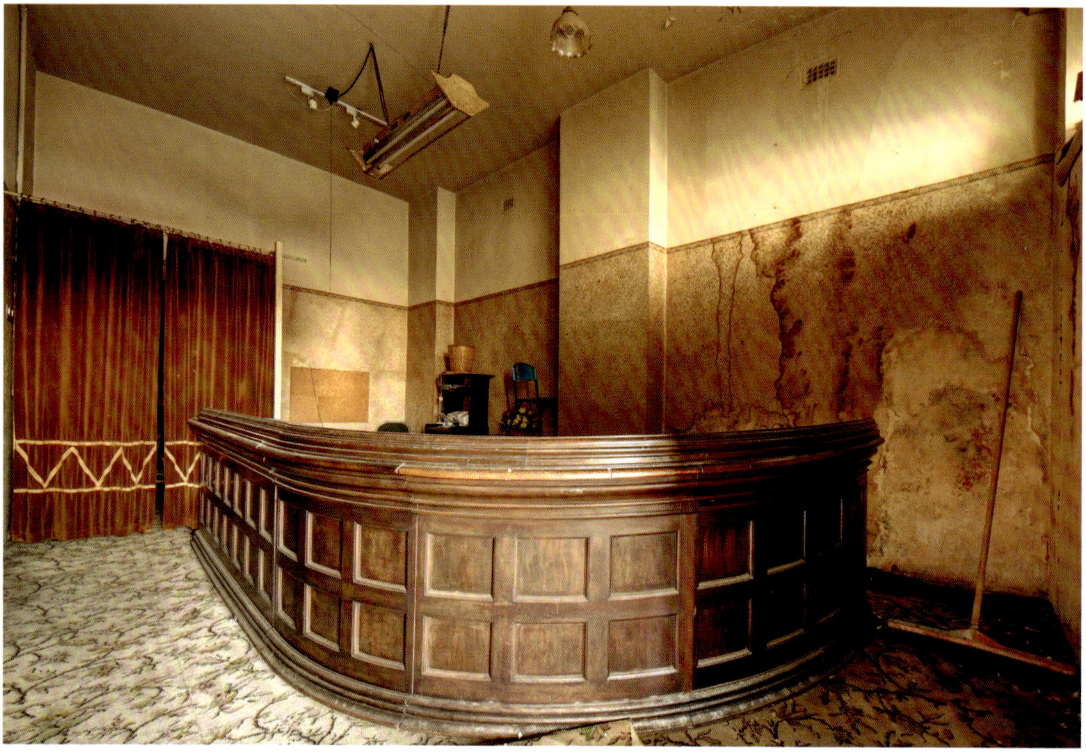

The former cloakroom

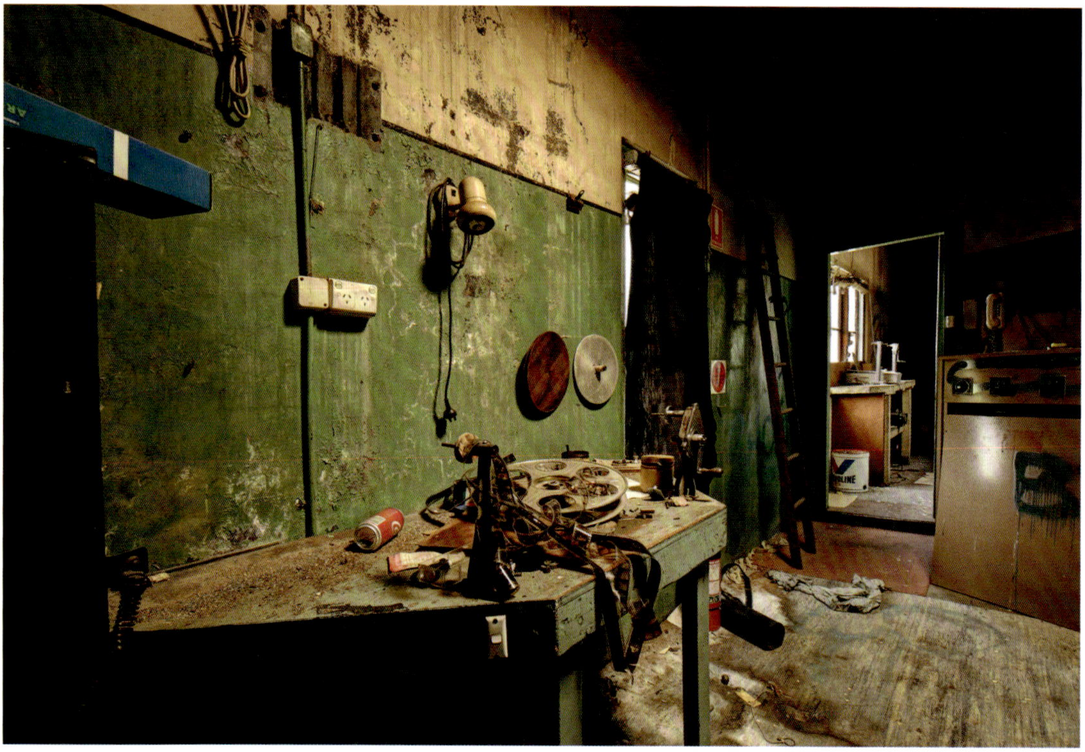

The narrow projection room contains the relics of vintage cinematic days long since passed

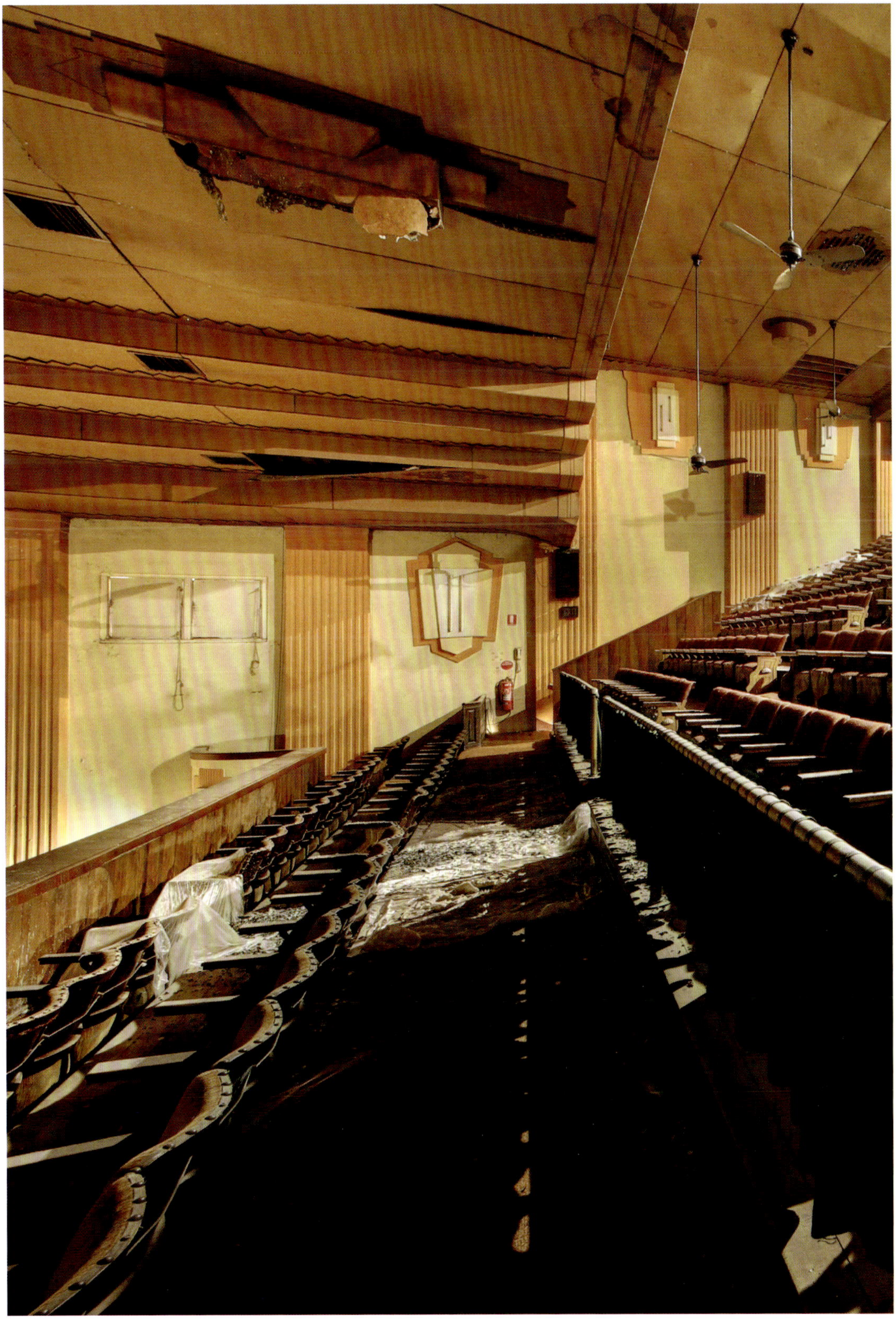

Rows of dust-covered seats align the upper balcony

ST JOHN'S ORPHANAGE

St John's Orphanage looms ominously over a raised suburban area in the township of Goulburn. Built in 1912, the facility operated initially as a home for 'wayward' boys. Later years would see its intake extend to girls as a result of a dwindling need to house homeless males, who were perhaps viewed as useful farmhands and put to work as agricultural labourers. Governed by the Catholic Church, the orphanage provided displaced and unwanted youths with a sternly religious and agricultural education.

Inside, a charred narrow staircase leads to the former nuns' quarters and bathrooms. A sinister energy hangs heavy within the gloomy structure. Known for its dark and contentious past, previous residents often speak of the abuses they endured whilst housed at St John's.

Closing in 1978, all last remaining residents were placed in homes in surrounding townships. The following year, a youth missionary organisation commenced governance of the property. In 1994, the facility was abandoned and has since fallen victim to a succession of incidents involving vandalism and fires. In 2015 a large blaze resulted in the collapse of a huge chunk of the building's front facade, leaving one third of the former orphanage in ruins.

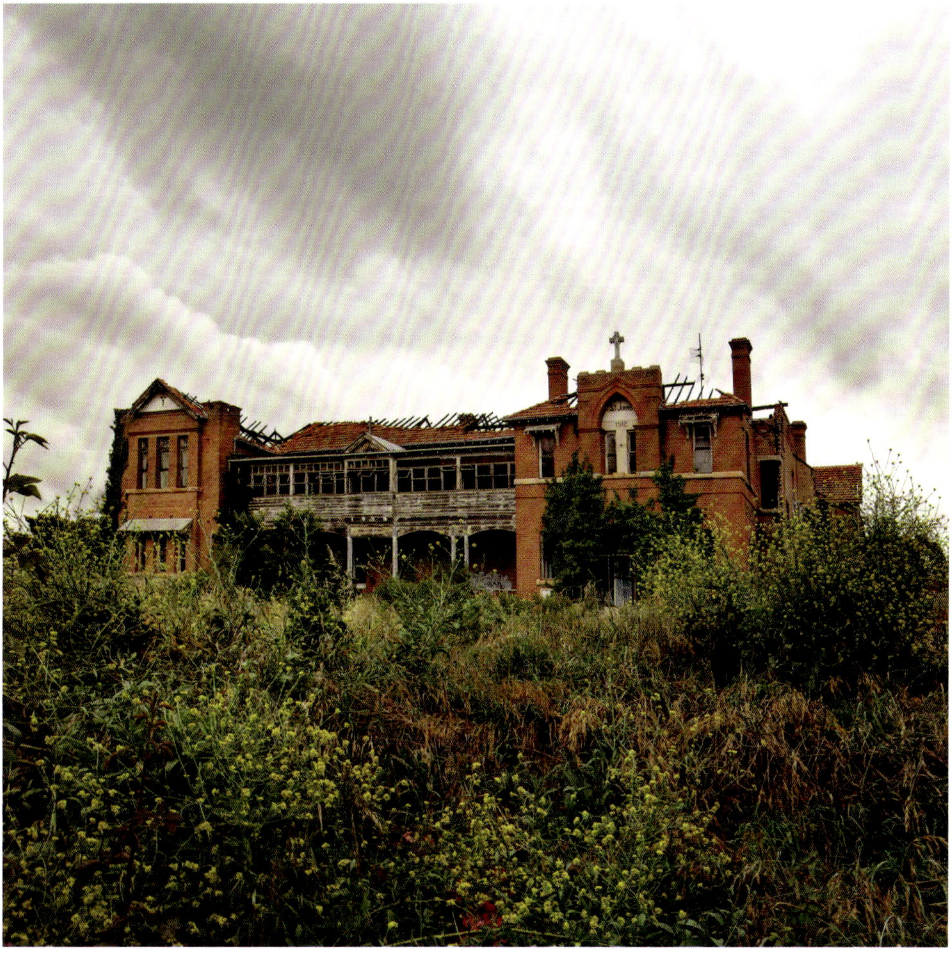

The remains of St John's Orphanage

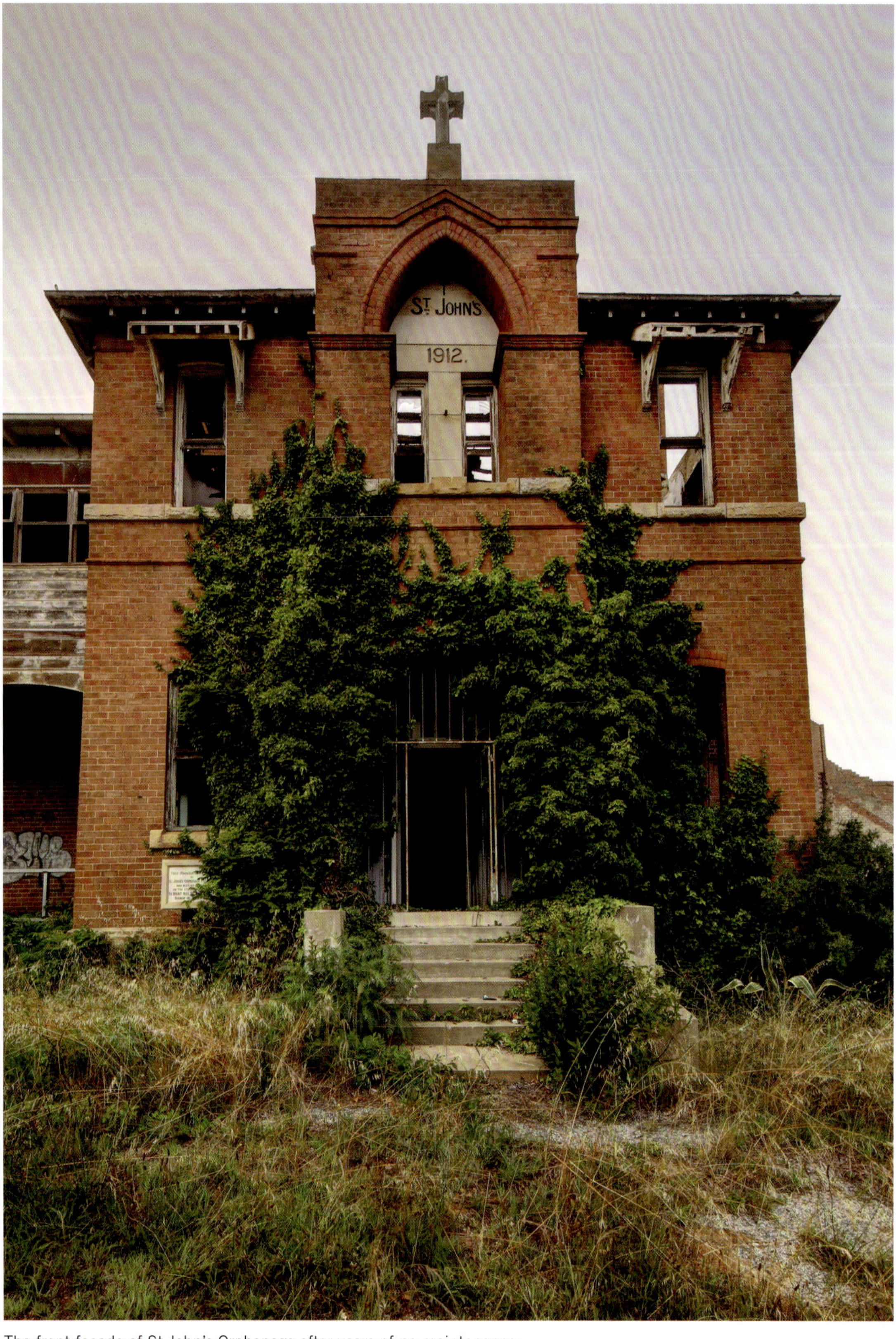

The front facade of St John's Orphanage after years of no maintenance

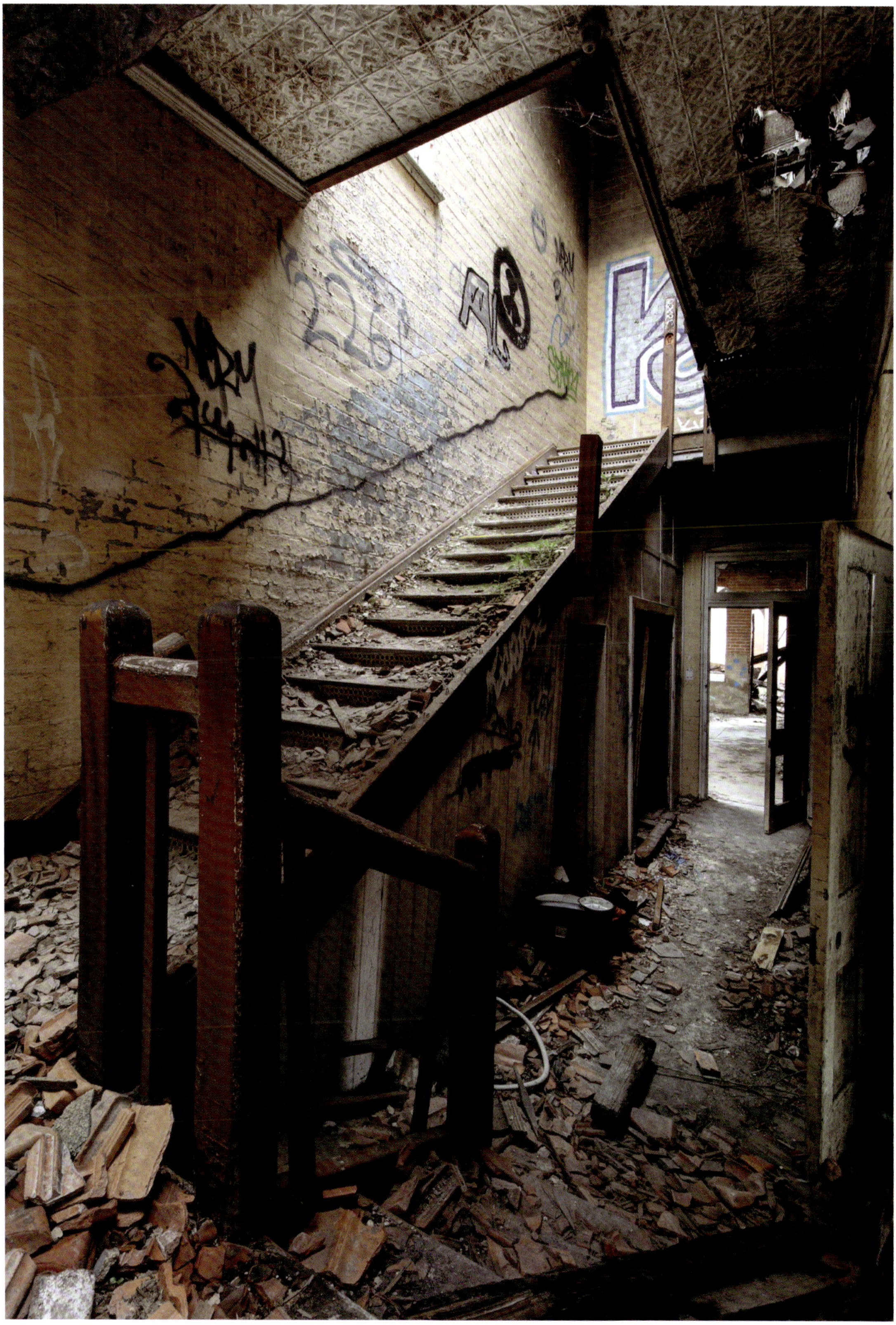

A debris-covered stairwell in the centre of the building

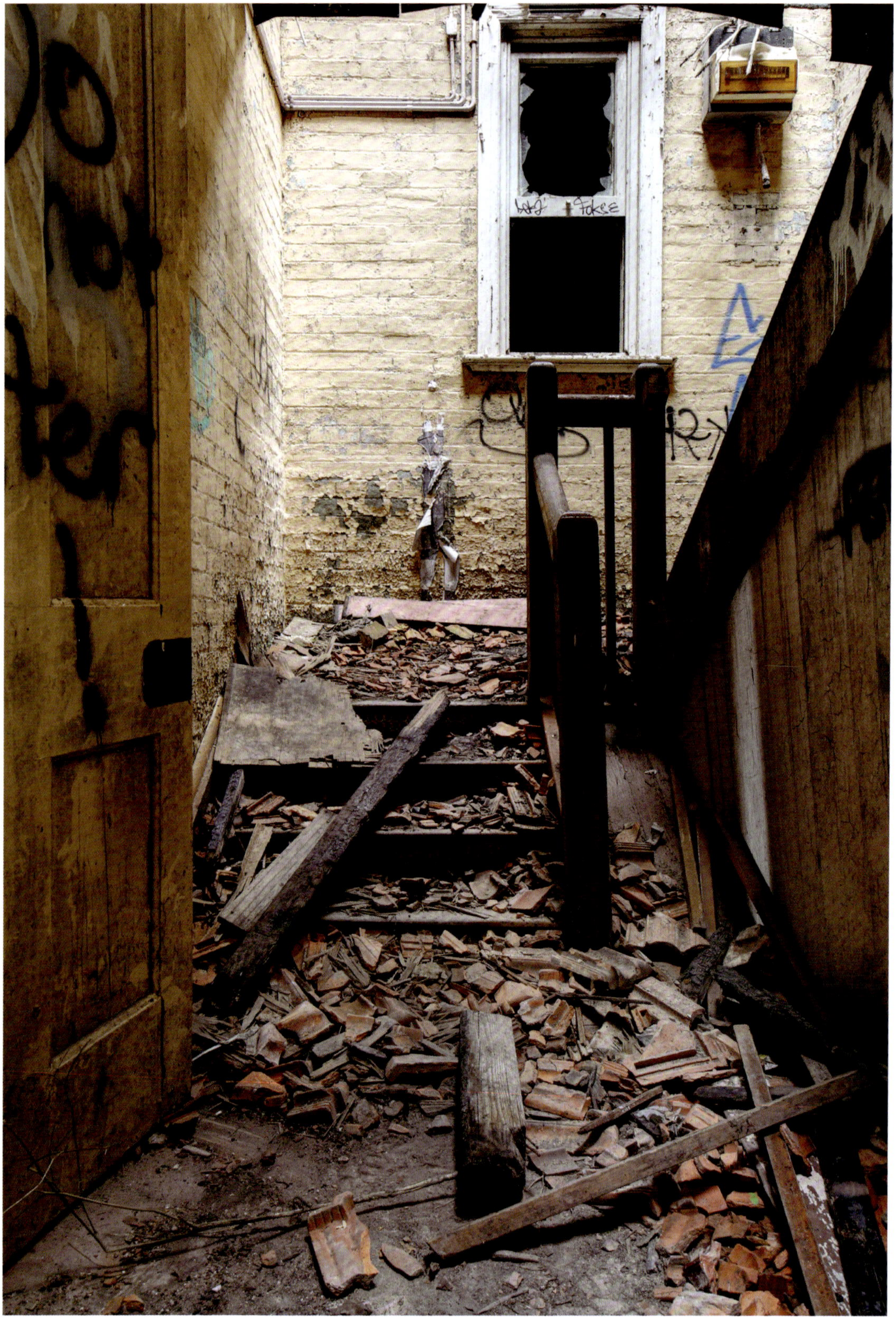
Stairs lead up to the facility's living quarters

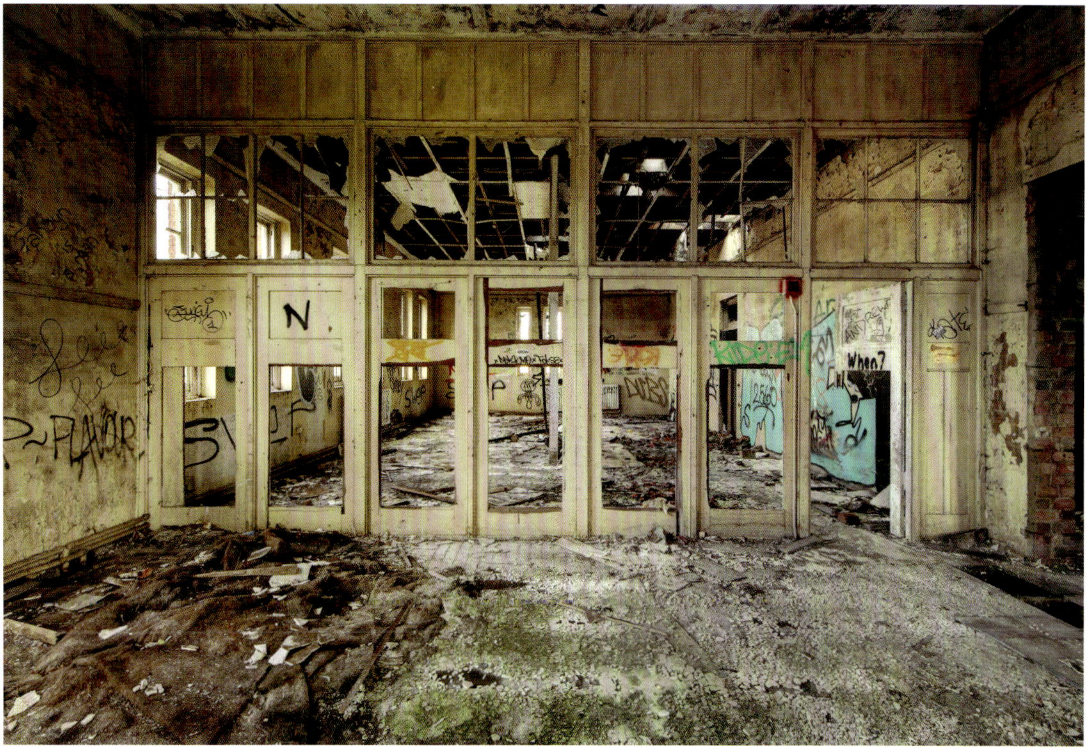

Years of vandalism has taken its toll

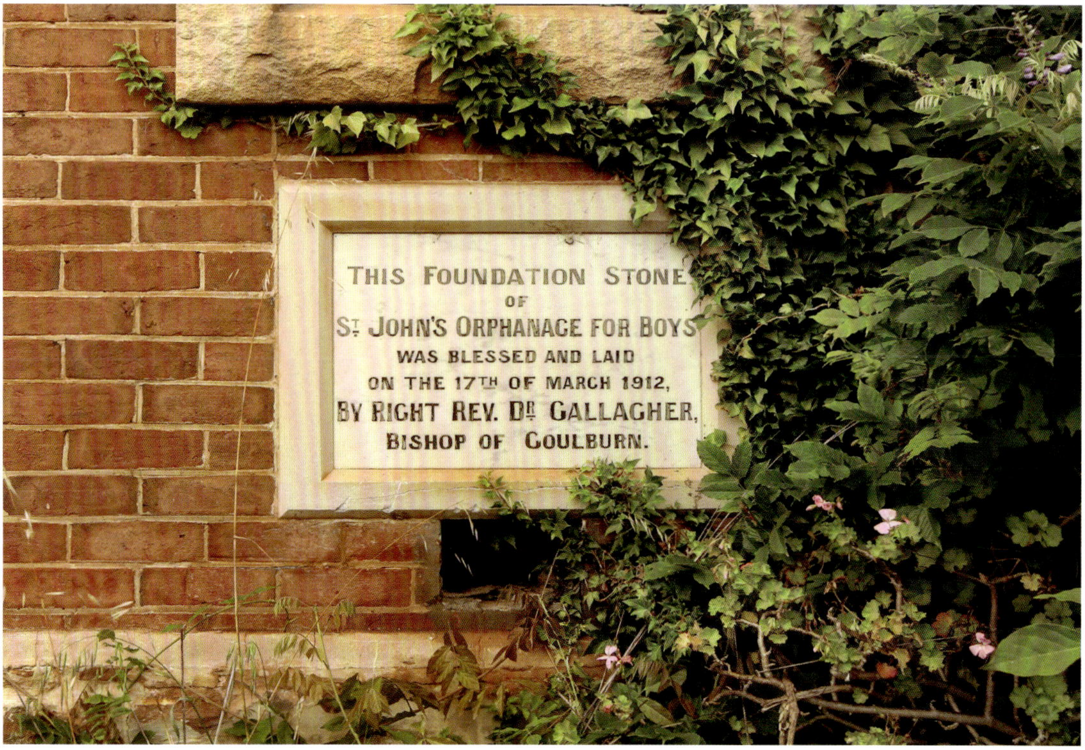

The original foundation stone, set in 1912

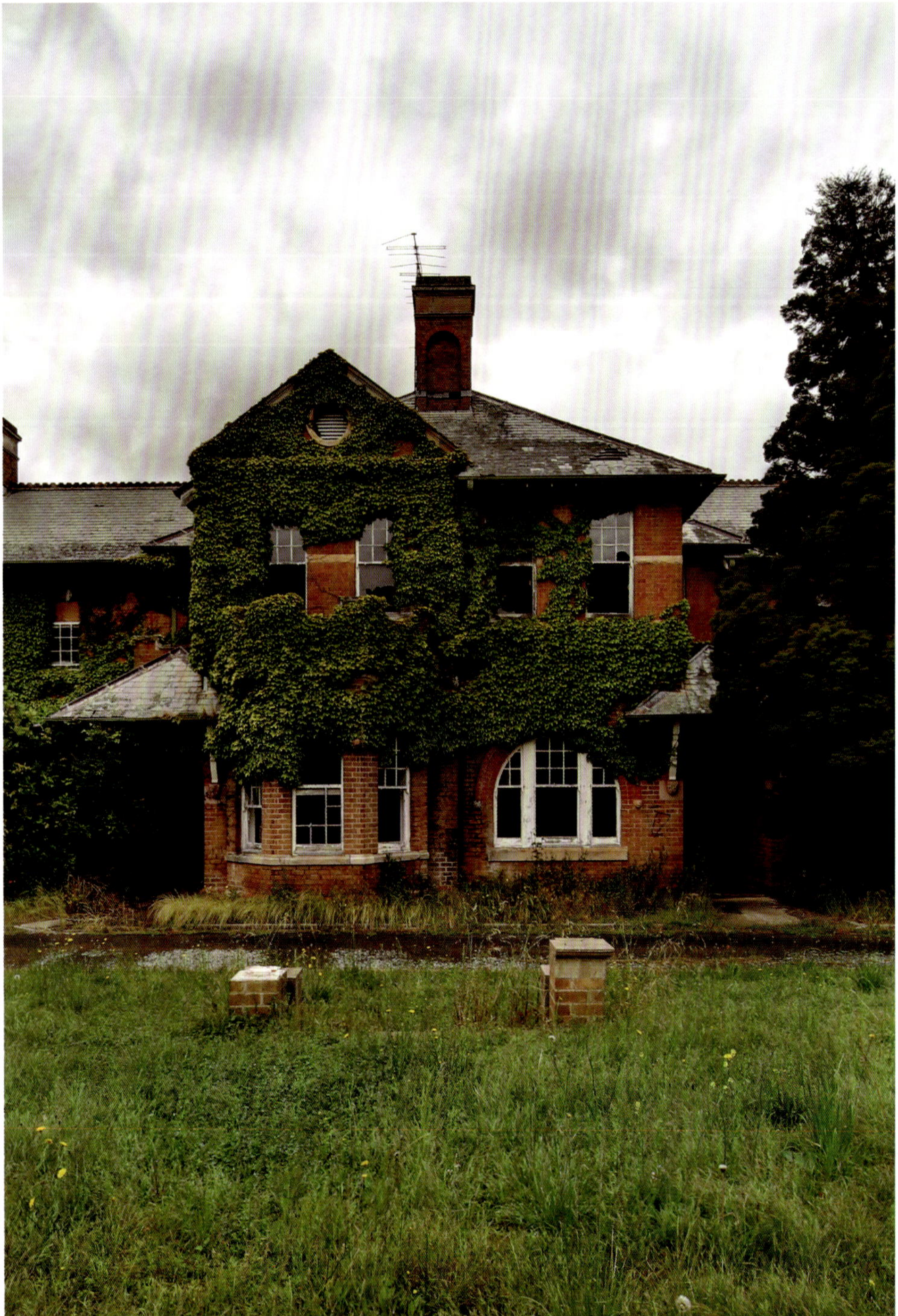

Kenmore facility's overgrown central building

THE ASYLUM

Holding the unenviable title of one of Australia's most supposedly haunted locations, Kenmore Asylum opened officially in 1895. By 1897, 192 patients were housed at the large complex. Capable of accommodating up to 700 people, the war period saw the facility transformed into a military hospital, thus pushing most of its existing patients to various asylums closer to Sydney.

Housing people with a range of illnesses and traits considered socially impermissible at the time, the years leading up to the 1940s would see the hospital suffer a succession of ill-fated events. In 1902, a patient hung himself with a strip of canvas rug tied to a window shutter. The following year, a patient suffocated during an epileptic seizure. Six years later, an inmate would be struck on the head by a rock flung from the hand of a resident prone to violent outbursts. The next decade would add another suicide to the asylum's grim tally after a patient hung himself from a tree in the midst of a depressive episode.

Further woes were to occur in 1919 when a pneumonic influenza killed 21 patients, most likely attributable to the deadly Spanish Flu pandemic encompassing the world at that time. Continuing the hospital's melancholic timeline, a woman was violently murdered at the hands of her husband on the asylum's grounds in 1920.

Over the years since closure, numerous redevelopment plans have been proposed. However, the owners are yet to decide whether these lavish grounds will be re-zoned as a retirement precinct or perhaps an educational facility. Given its dark and contentious past, the ominous cloud hovering over this space may never lift.

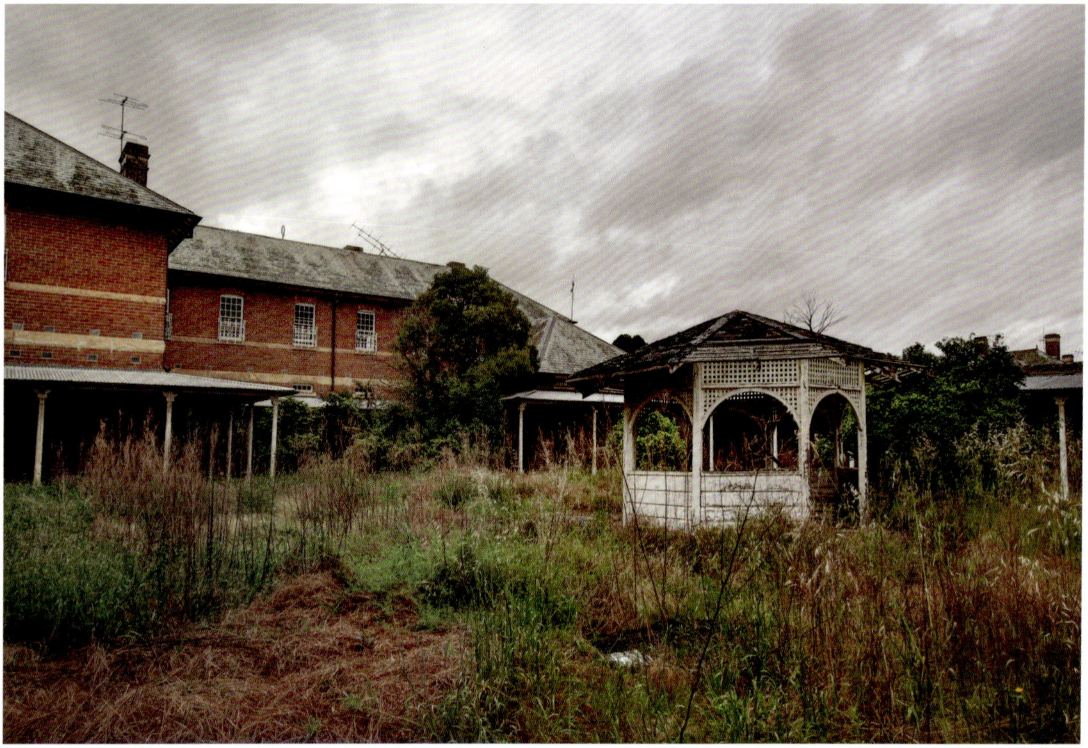

A gazebo in an overgrown garden space

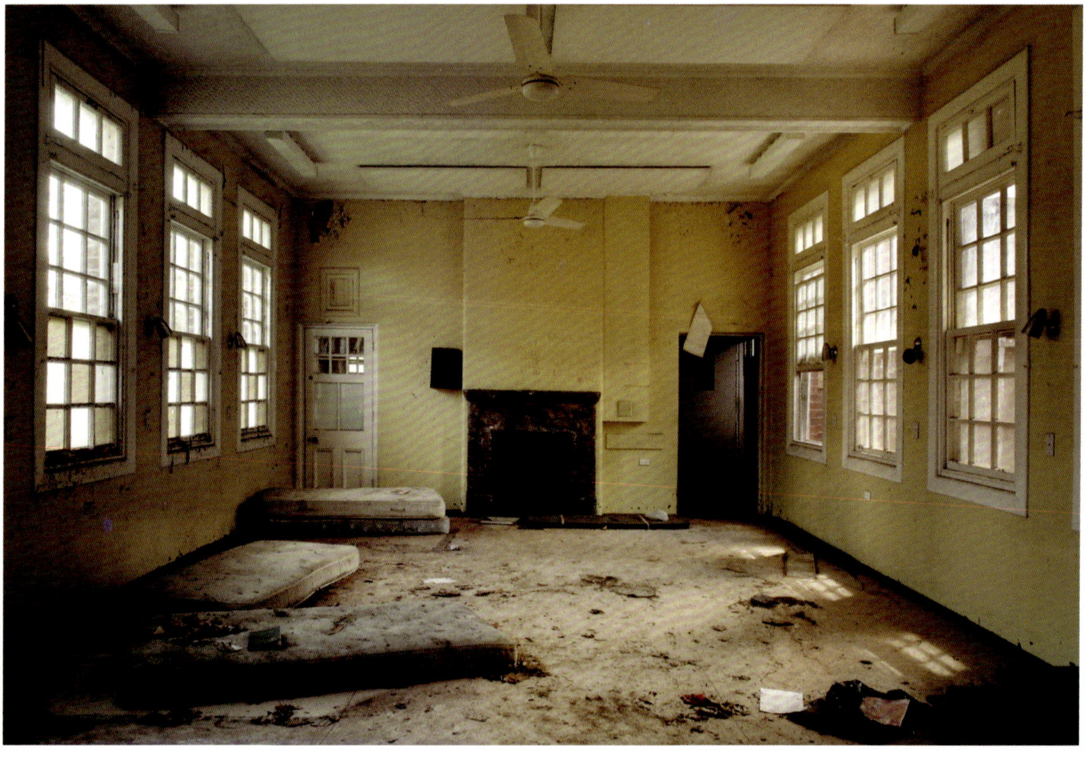

Mattresses line the floors of an empty ward

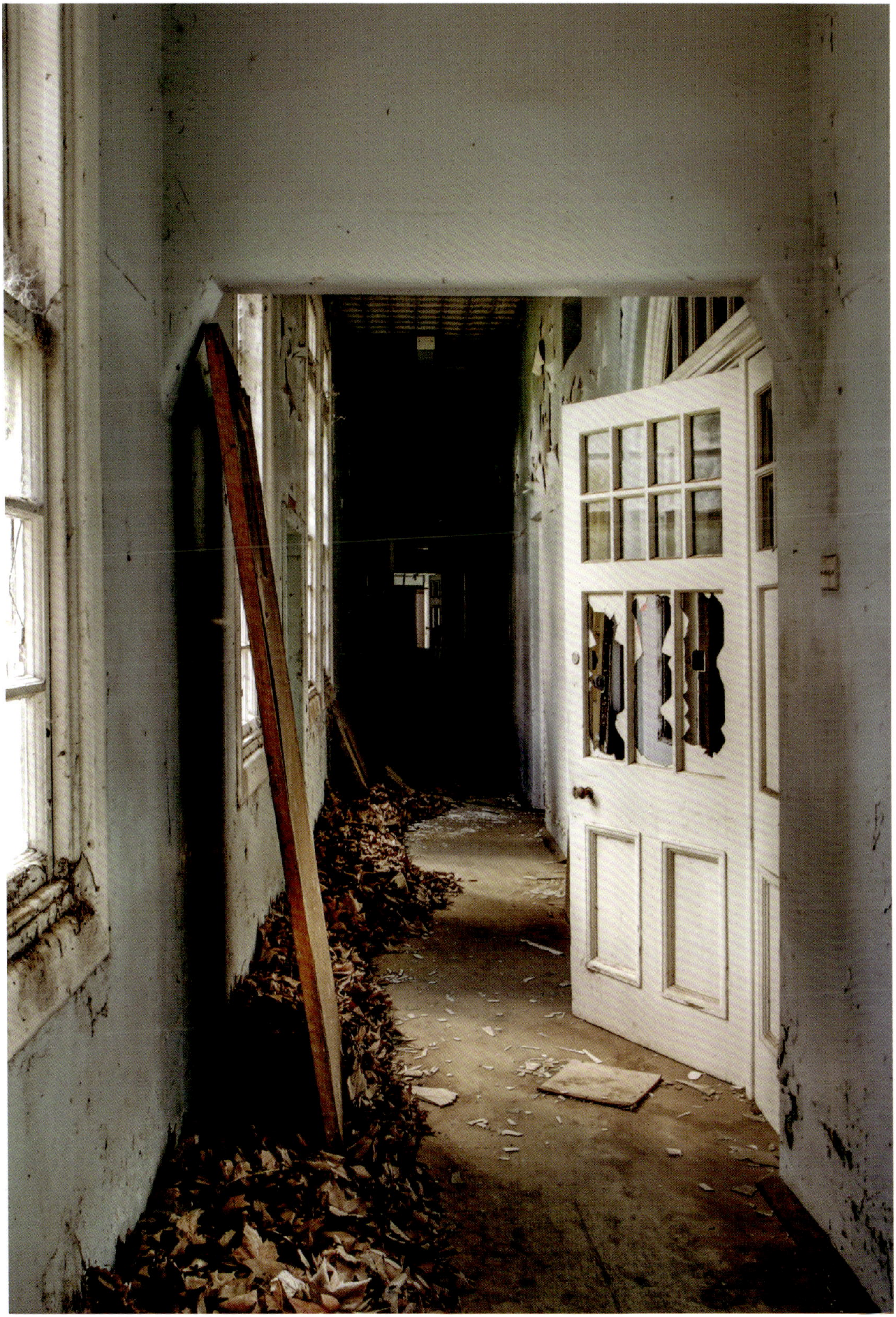

The asylum is filled with gloomy passageways that lead into darkness

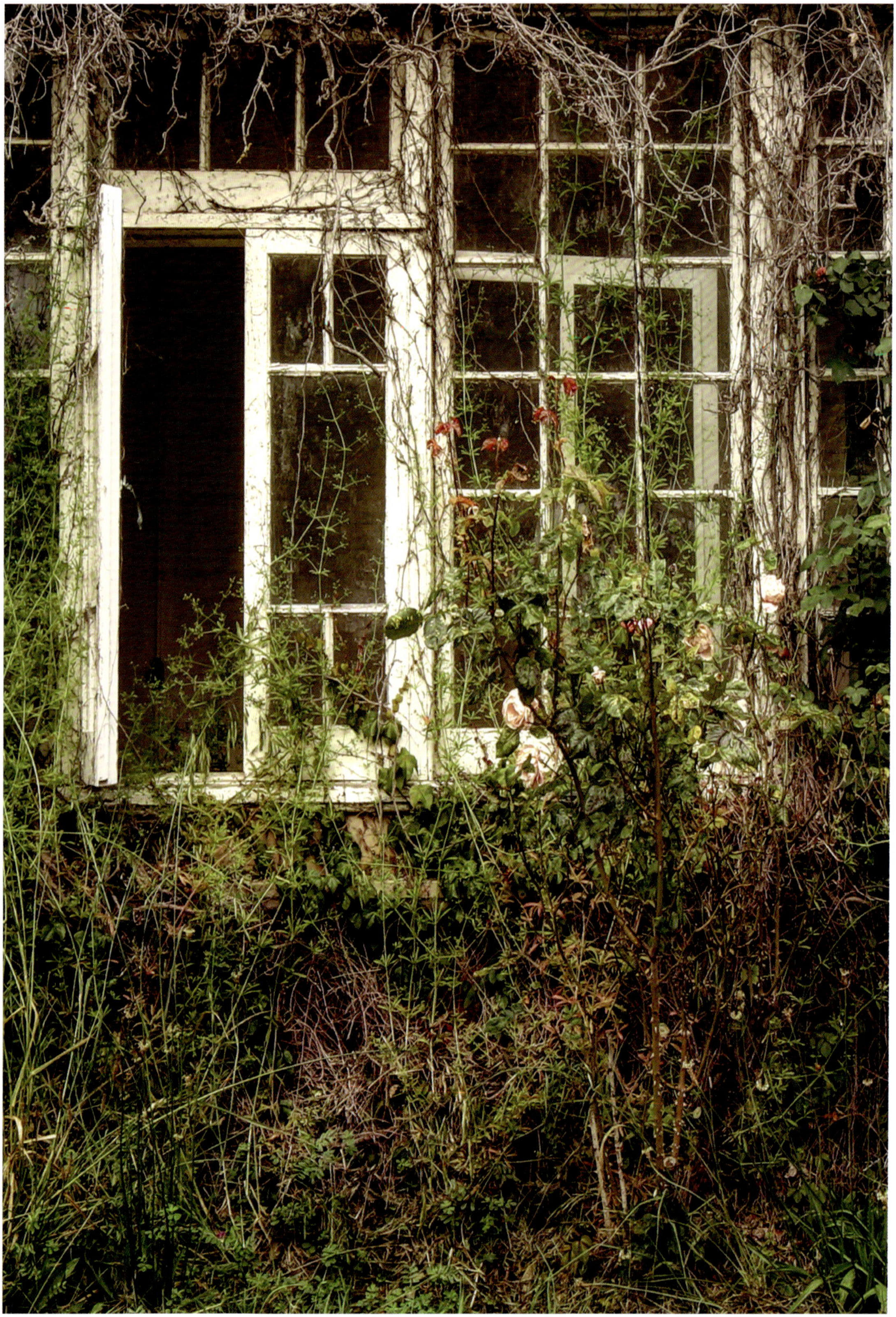

Flowers and foliage invade the asylum

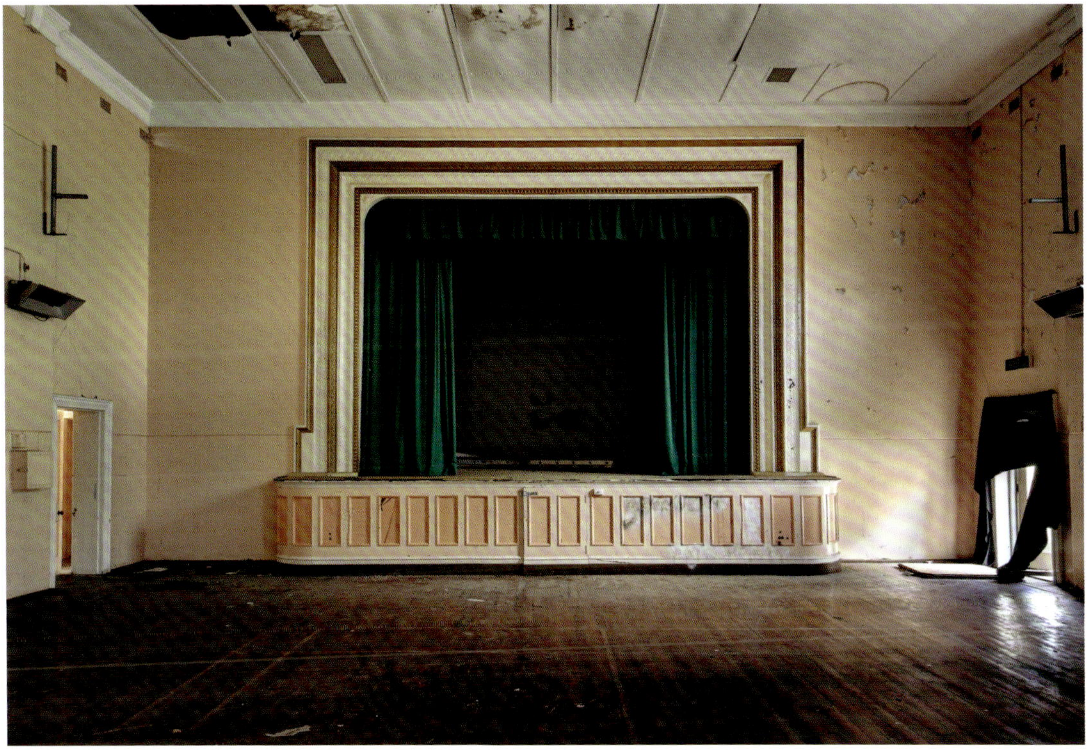

A stage sits at the end of a large hall

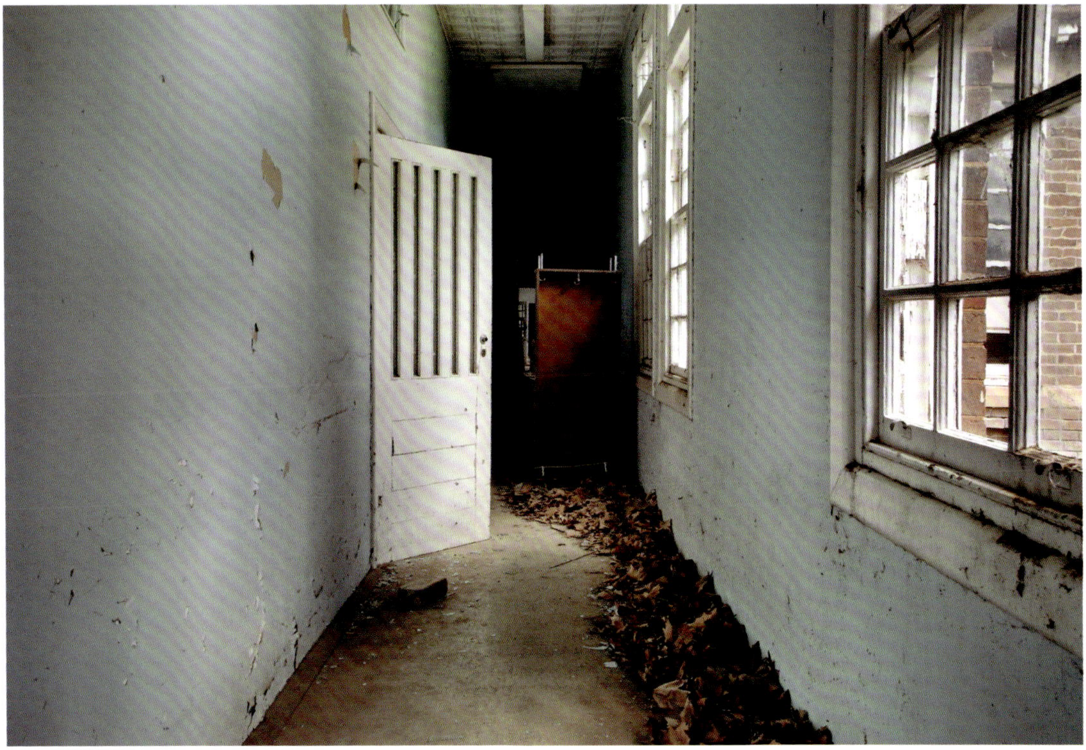

A dark passageway lined with patient observation cells

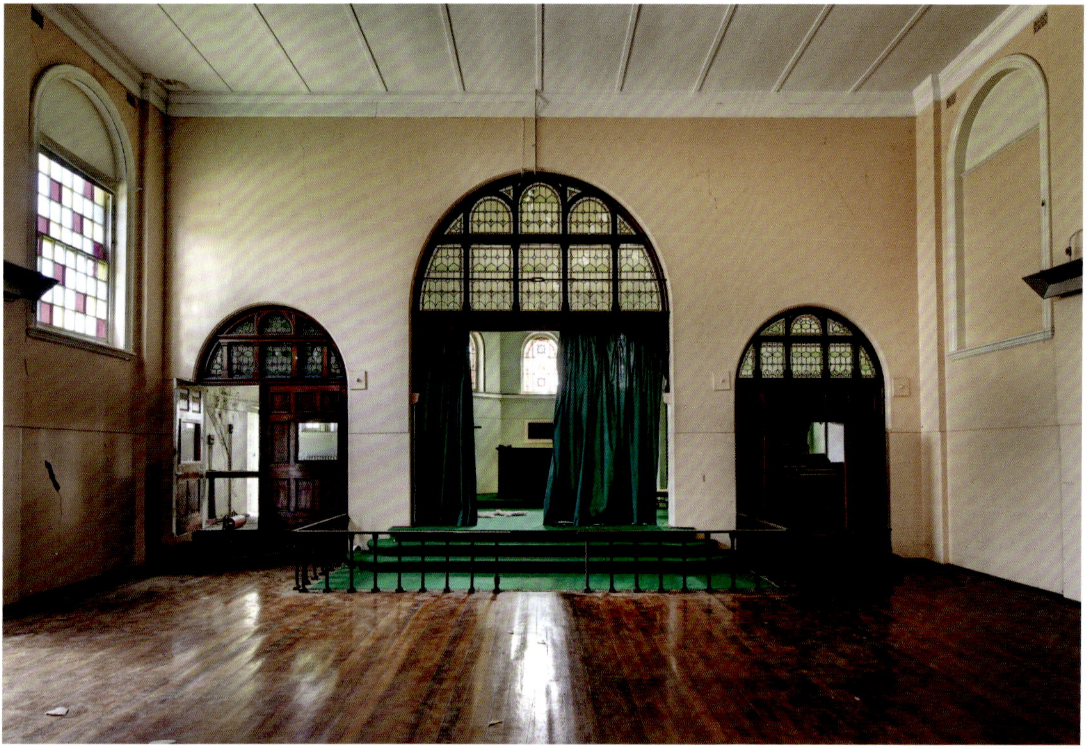

The community hall has since been vandalised

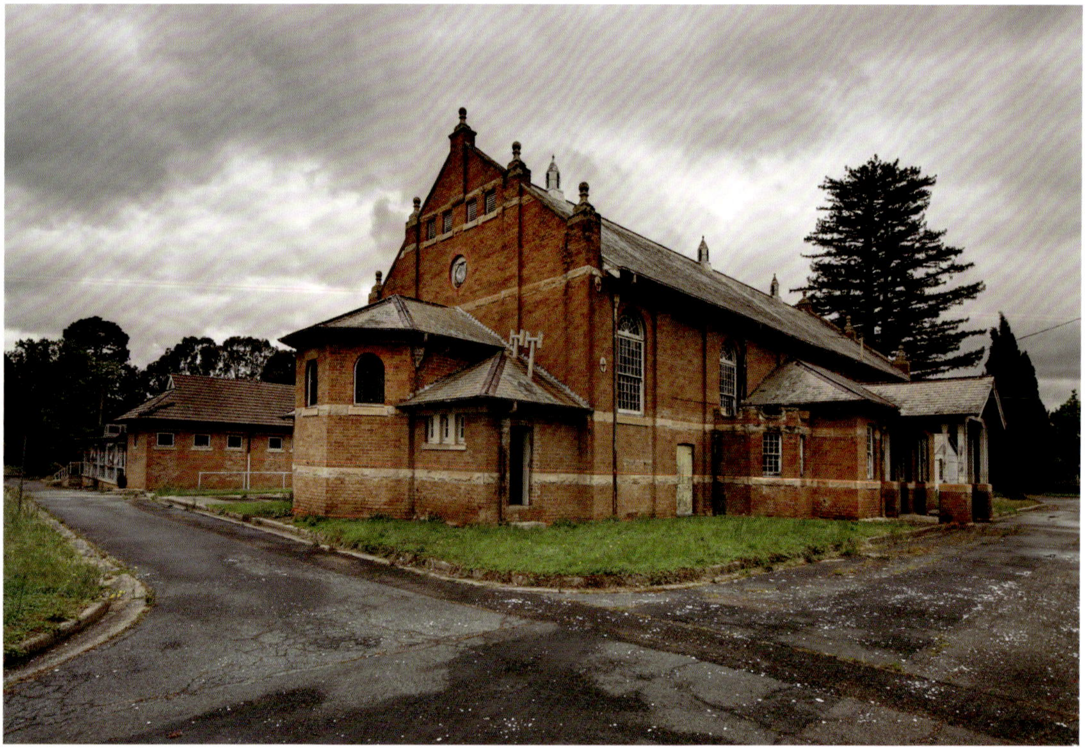

An exterior shot of the asylum's main hall

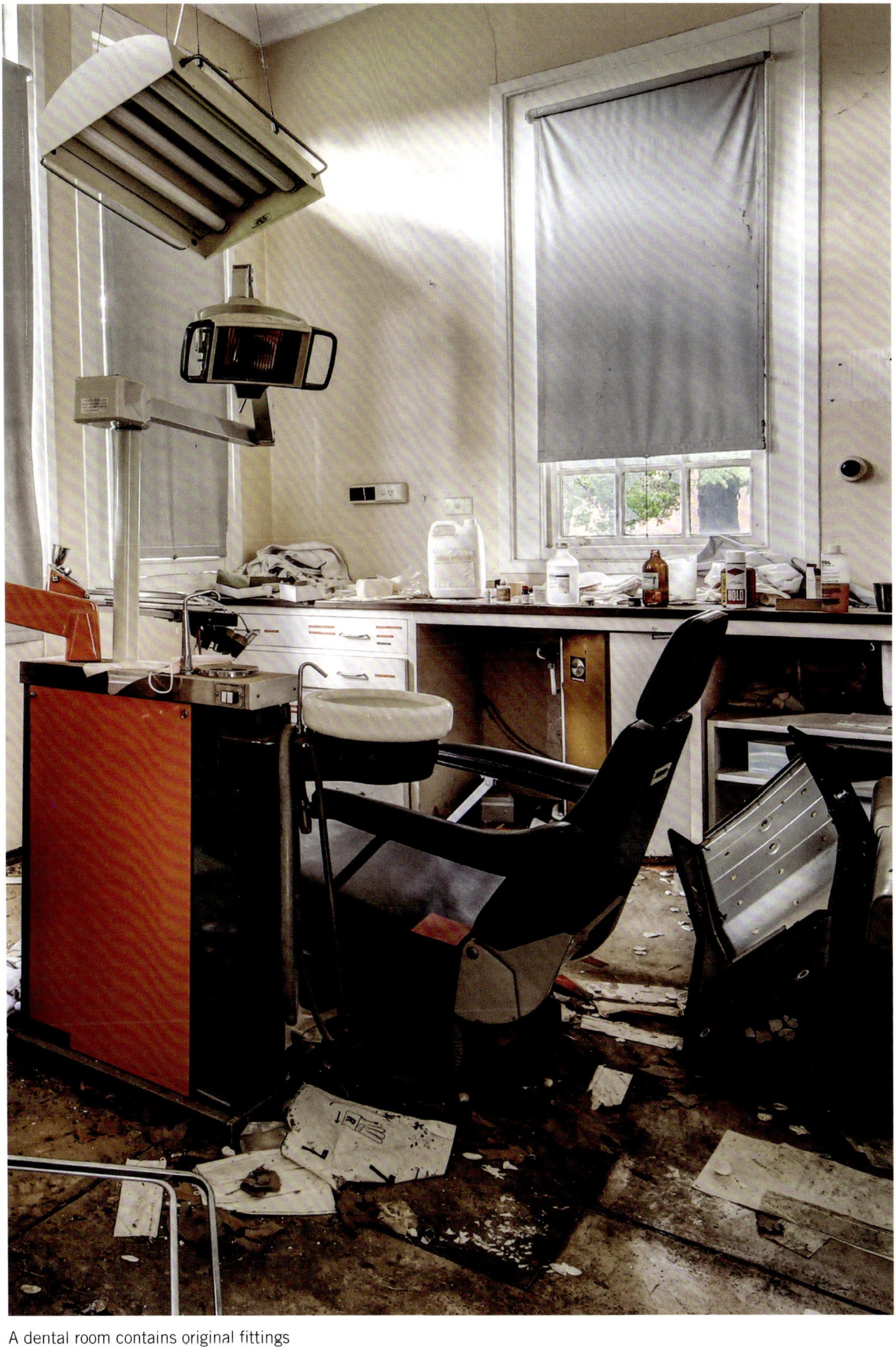

A dental room contains original fittings

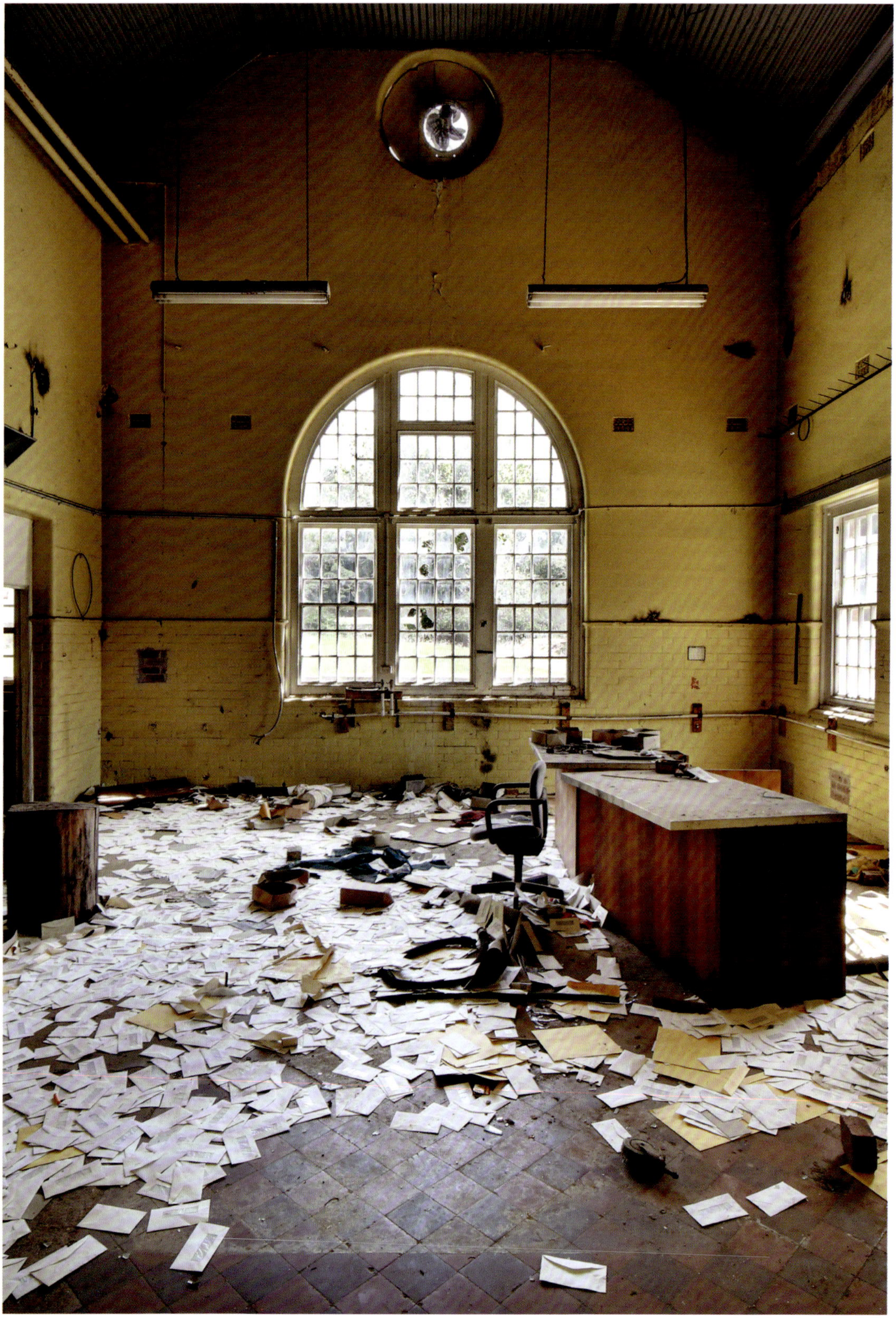

A littered office space

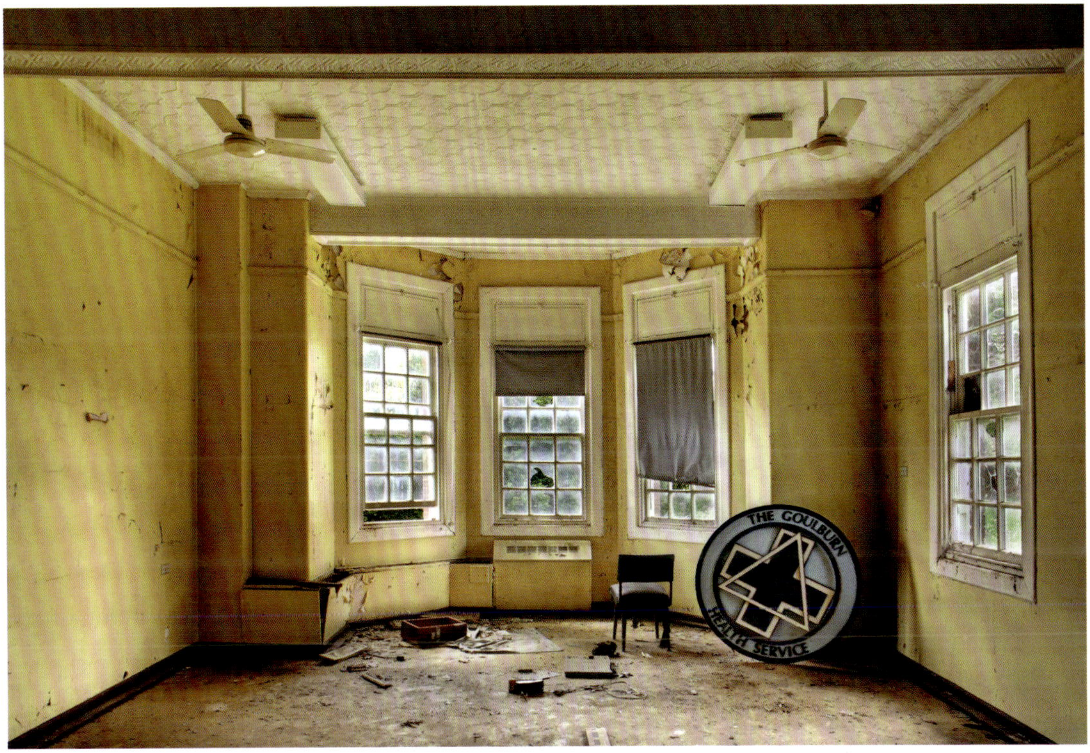

Another community room in the asylum

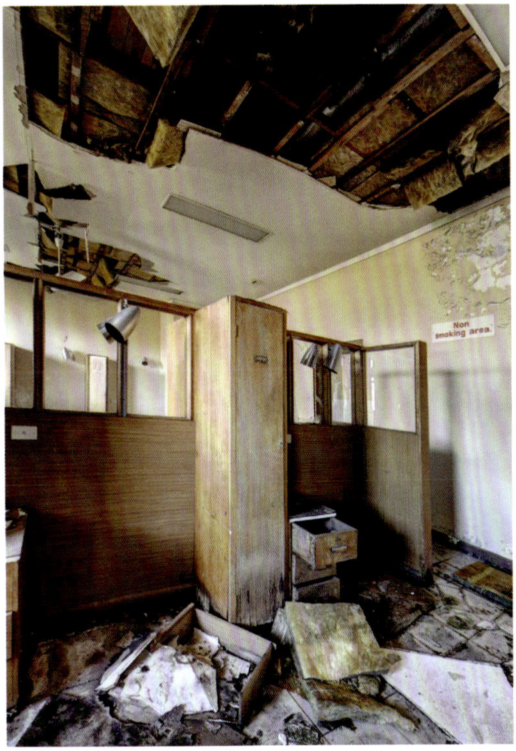

A dilapidated triage area

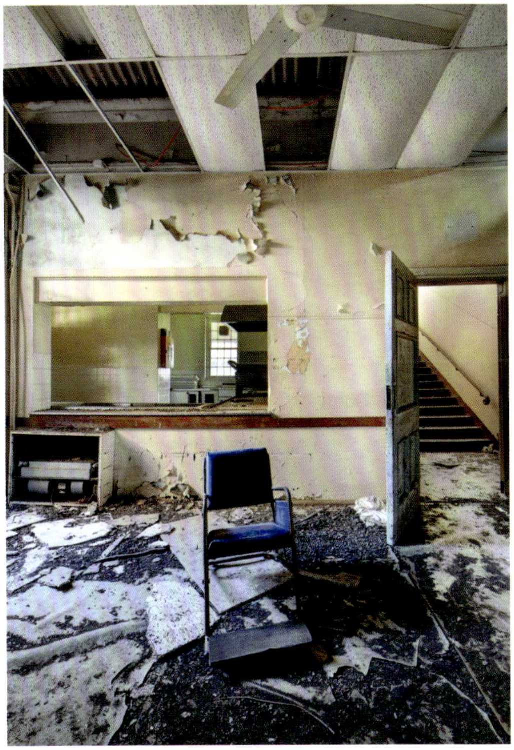

A crumbling communal patient space

WILCANNIA CONVENT

The traditional home of the Barkindji people, the desert township of Wilcannia sits on the infamous Barrier Highway. Hidden and somewhat out of place within the community's crisscrossed urban grid are the crumbling remains of the former Sisters of Mercy convent. Built in 1894 from local sandstone, a decline in population resulted in the permanent closure of the facility.

Severely dilapidated after years of no maintenance, long-term abandonment has rendered the building irreparable. Filled with pigeon faeces, feathers and rotting floorboards, the only remaining relic is a crumbled wooden staircase that ascends to a second-story level, revealing a series of empty, roofless rooms.

In 2012, the owner of the structure formed a restoration working group with the Central Darling Shire and Heritage NSW. However, given the Convent remains in a state of ruin in Wilcannia's back streets, it appears any initiatives have long since stalled.

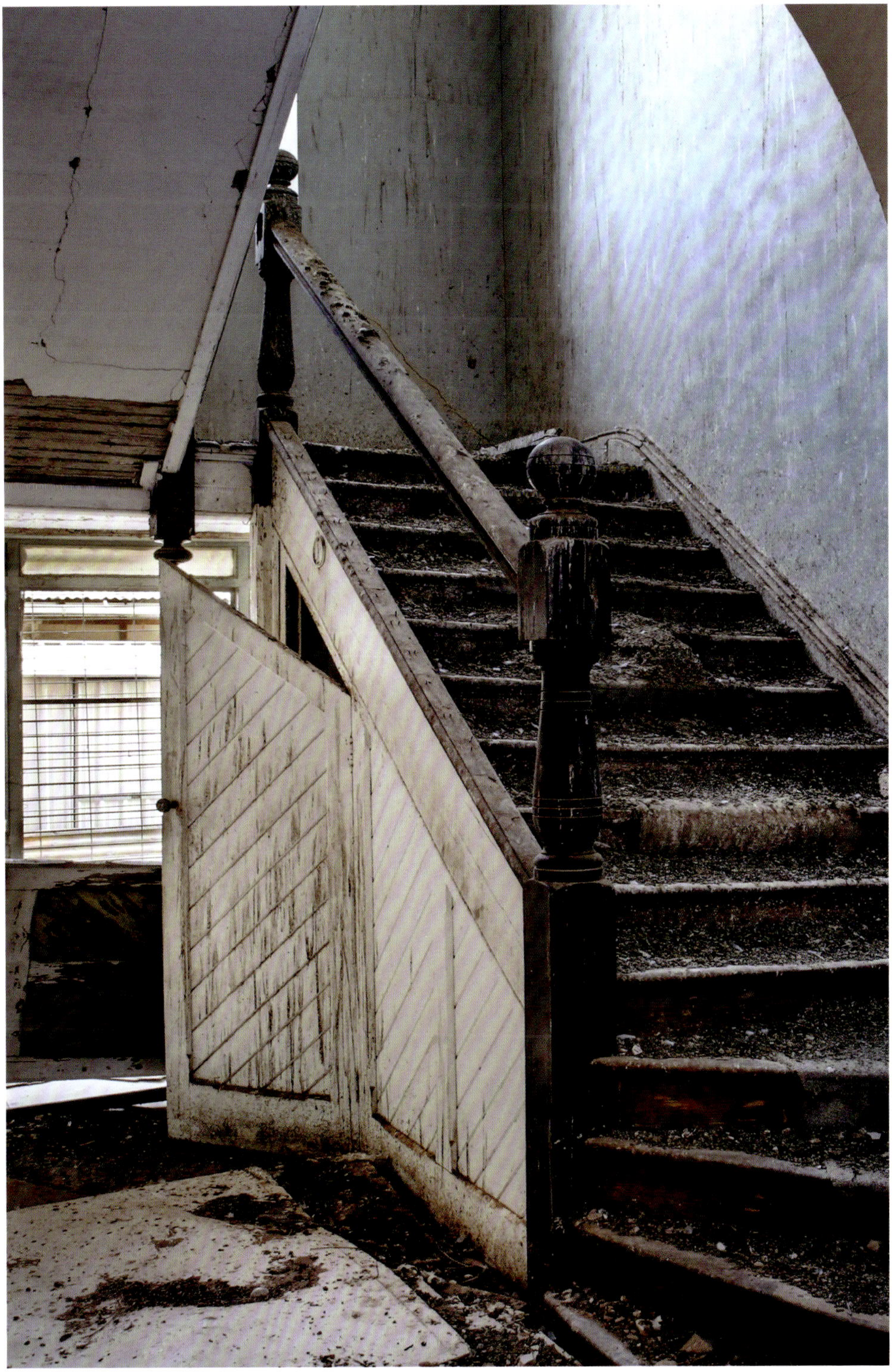

A dirt-covered stairway leads upwards to the roofless second floor of the convent

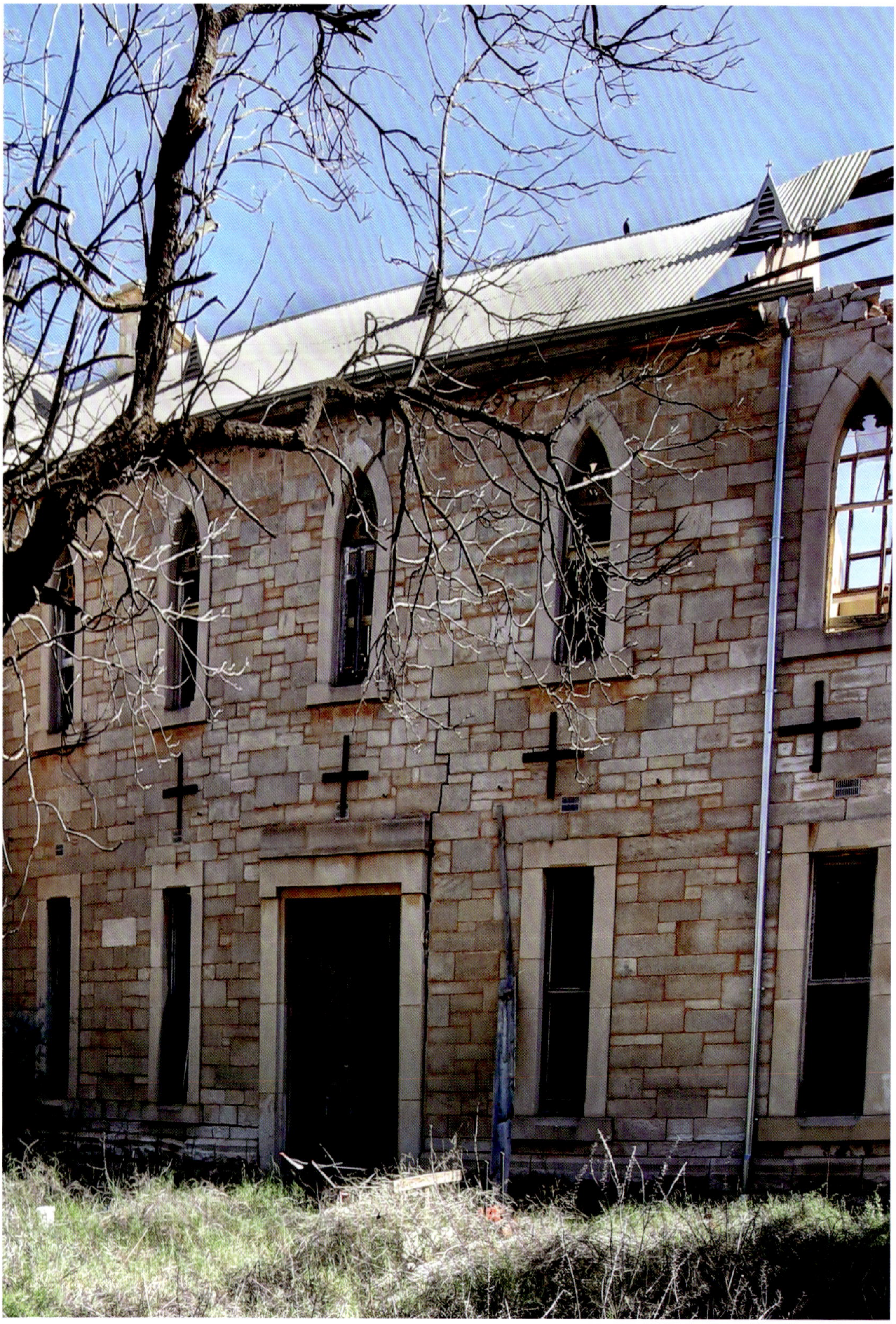

The front facade of the building shows cracks in the brickwork

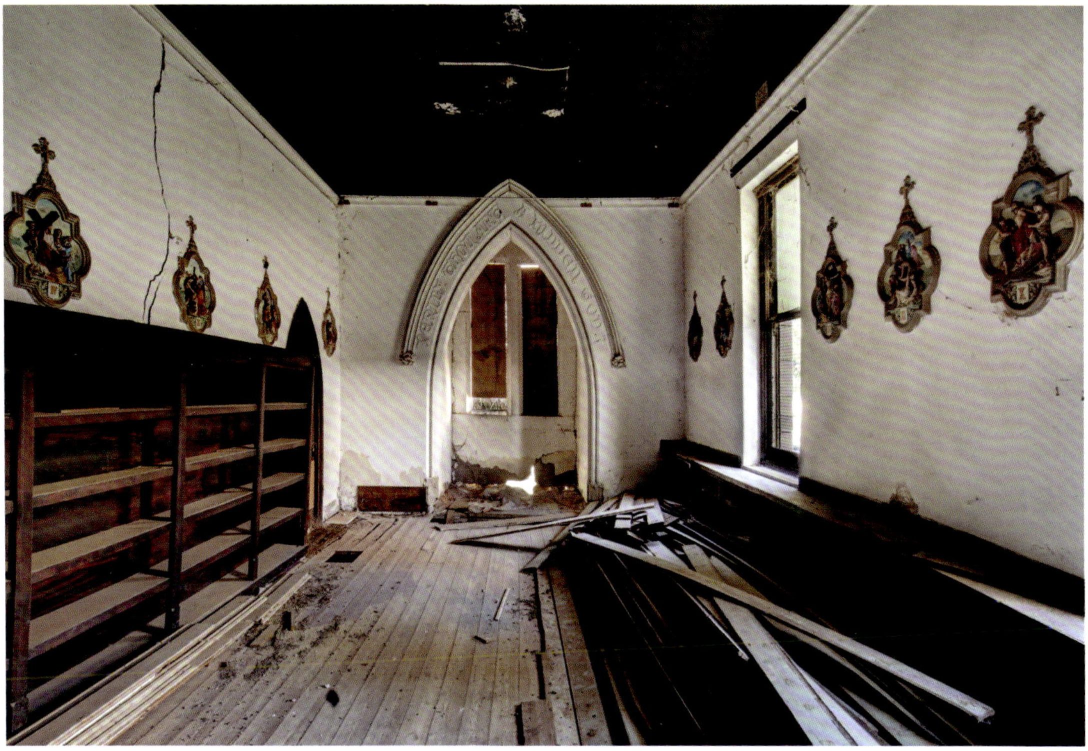

A former chapel

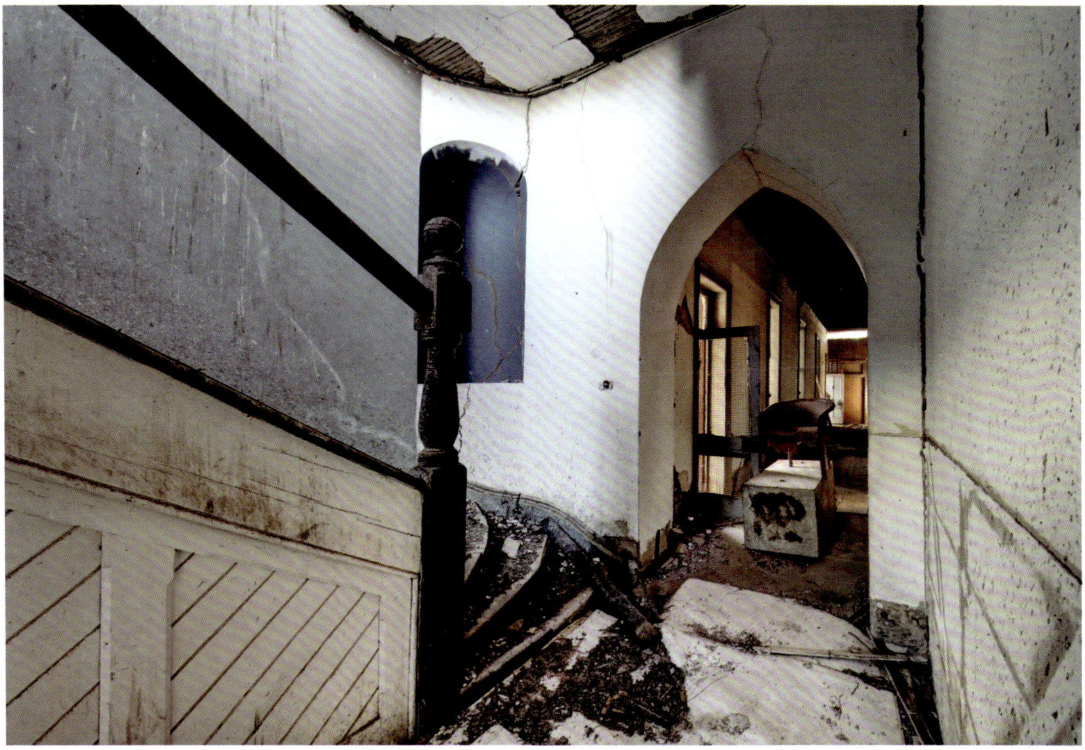

The stairwell leading to the convent's central hallway

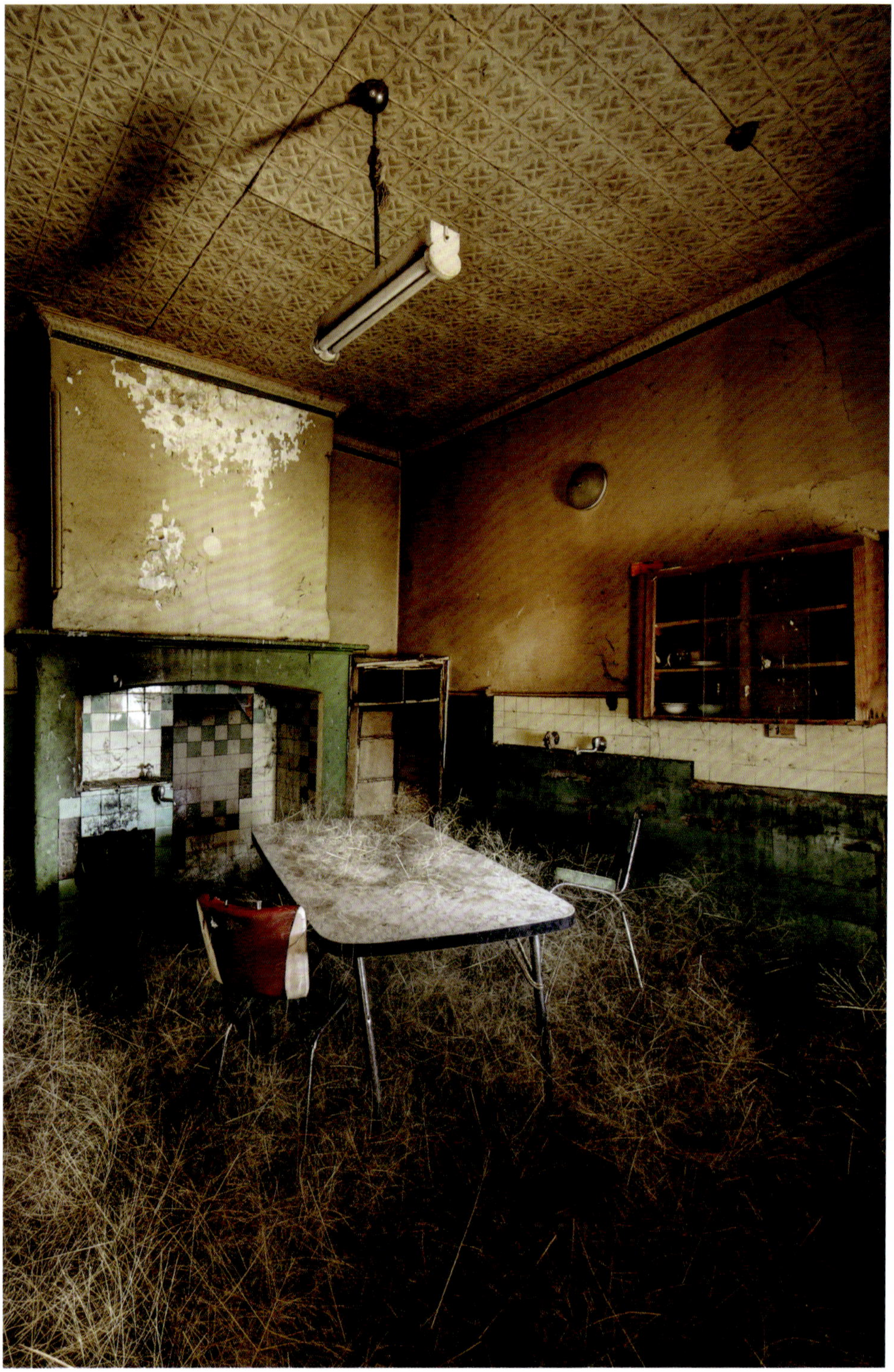

A former kitchen filled with *Panicum effusum*, known more commonly as 'Hairy Panic' weed

FARMHOUSES AND HOMESTEADS

Being left to ruin usually is the result of a newer residence being built elsewhere on a rural property. Discarded farmhouses can be found in all corners of the New South Wales landscape. Often re-utilised as storage spaces for agricultural tools, many remain furnished, creating an unintentional vintage time capsule. Speaking of lives once devoted to herding and harvesting, these humble spaces reflect the state's numerous flirtations with various post-colonial housing styles. From wartime to more recent architectural movements, their soft pastel walls and pressed tin ceilings usually remain intact.

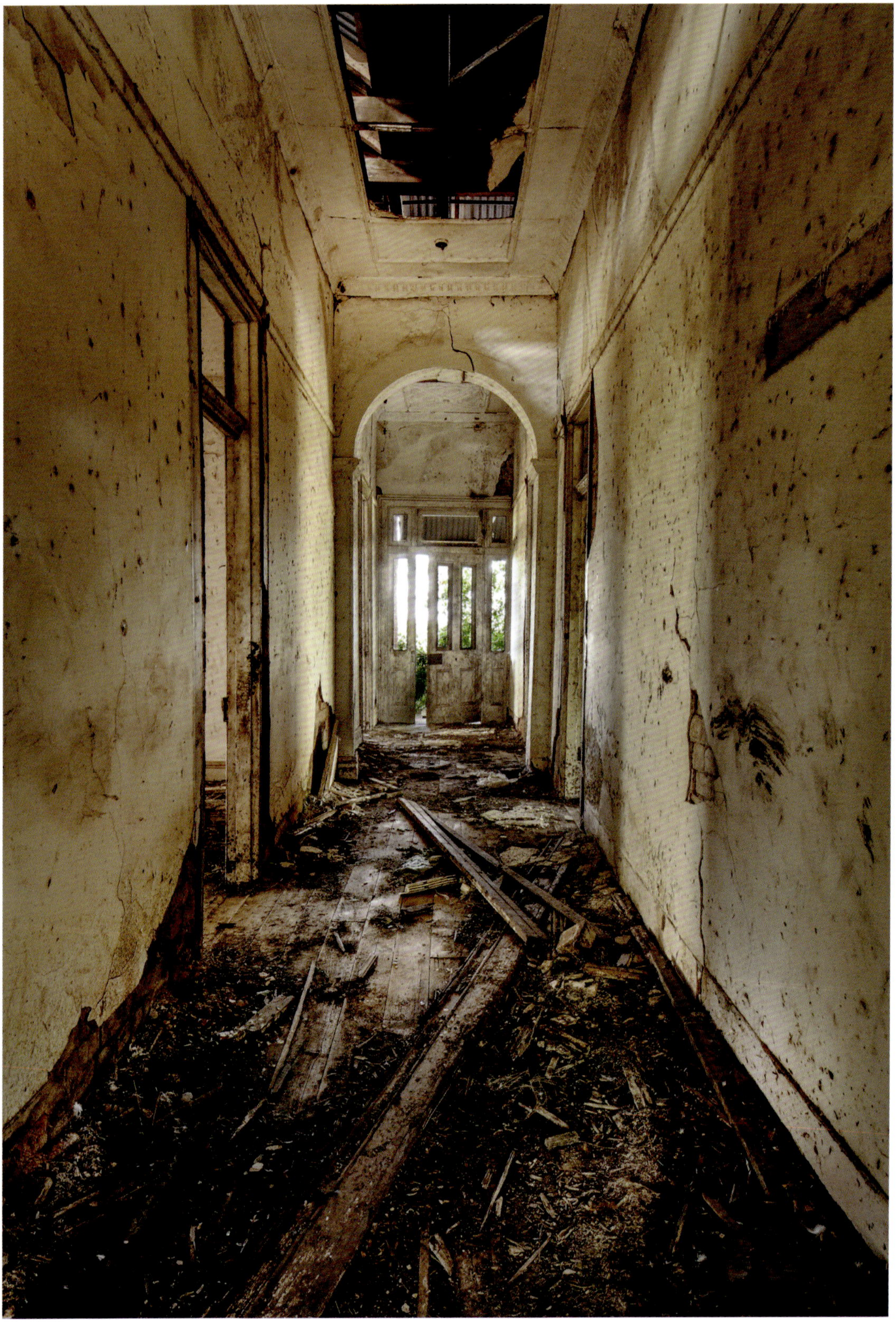

The dilapidated hallway of a former homestead in central NSW

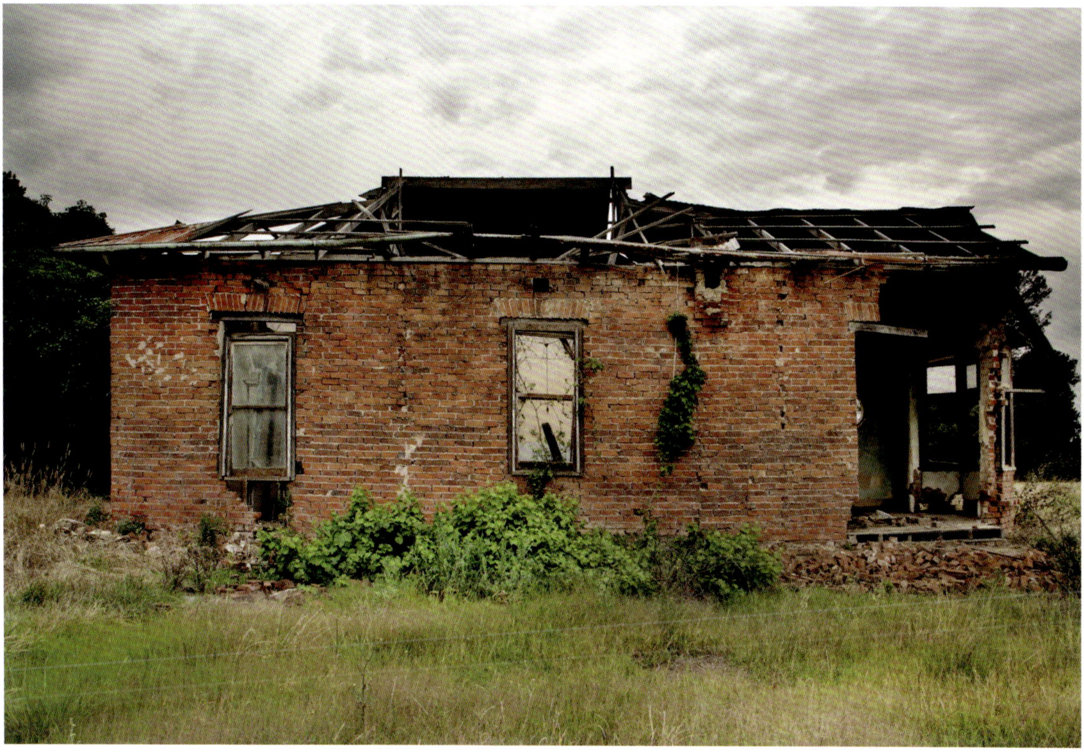

A crumbling farmhouse in Southern NSW

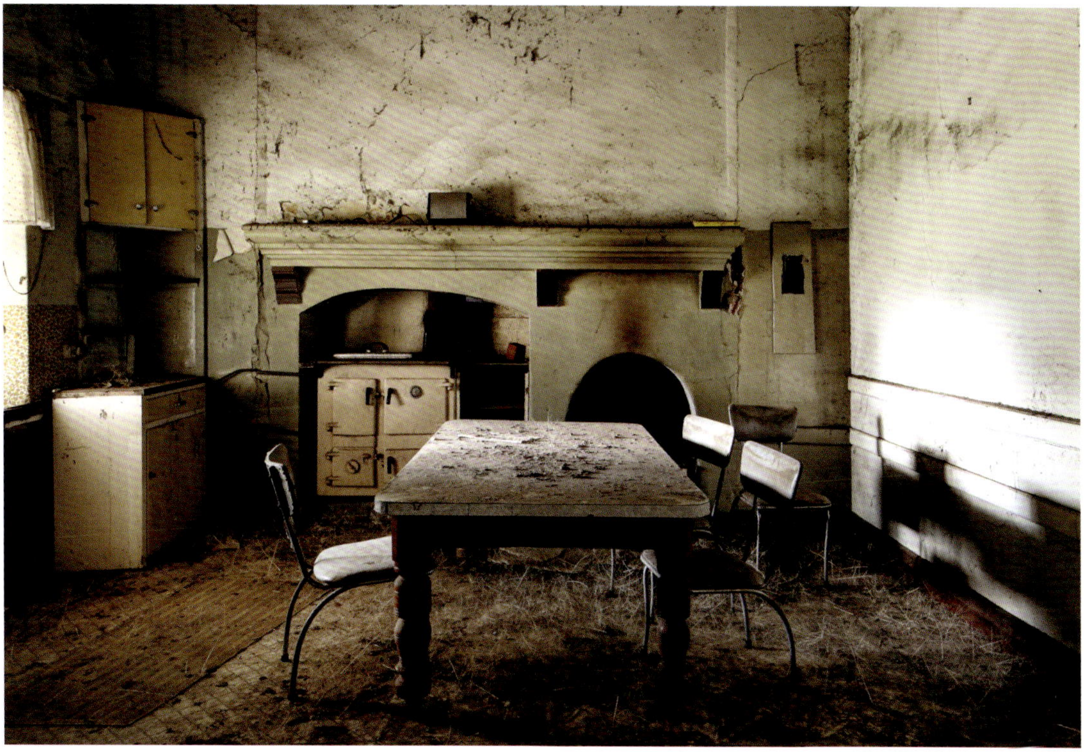

The smoke-stained kitchen of a former sheep station

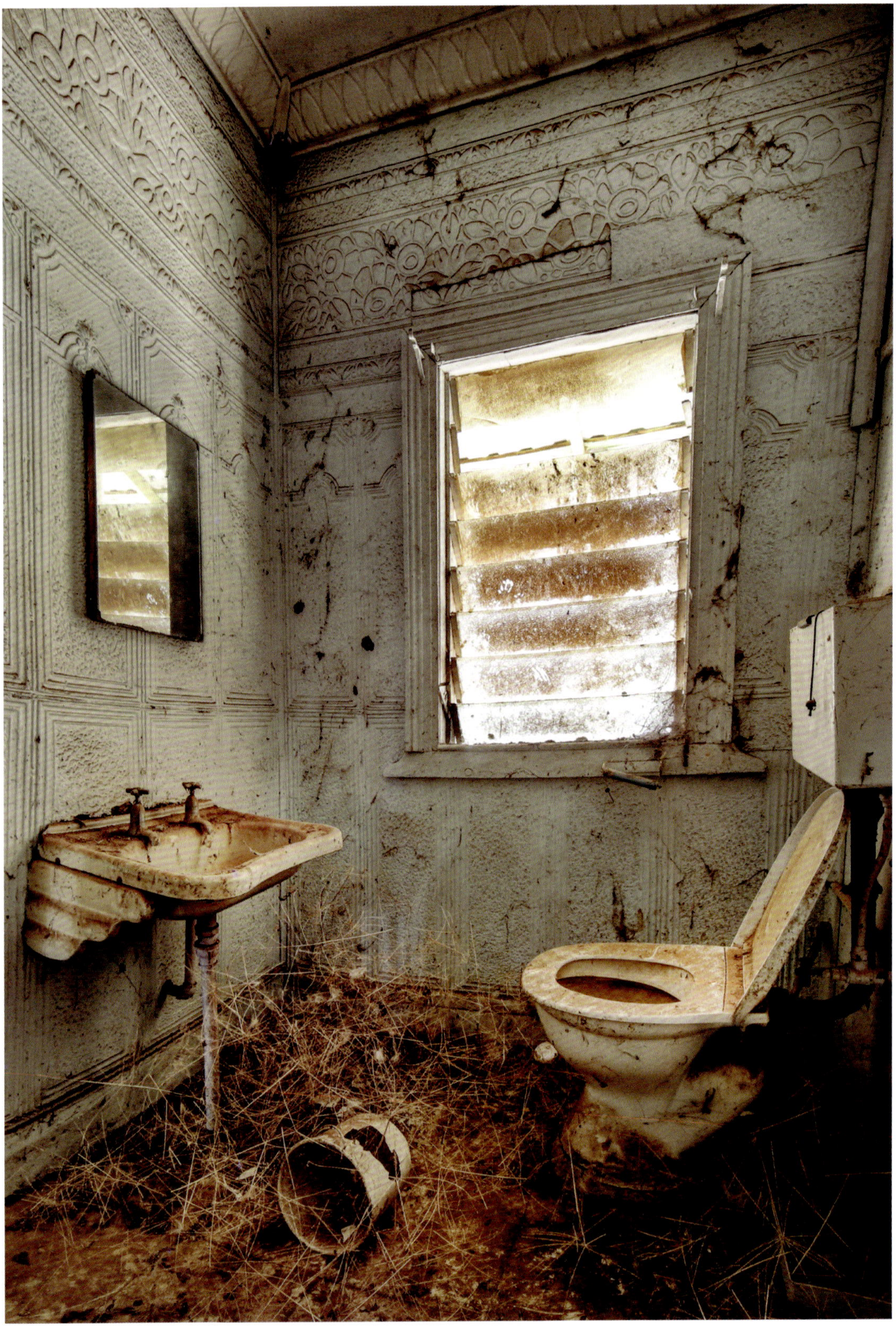

An Art Deco bathroom inside a former sheep station in southern NSW

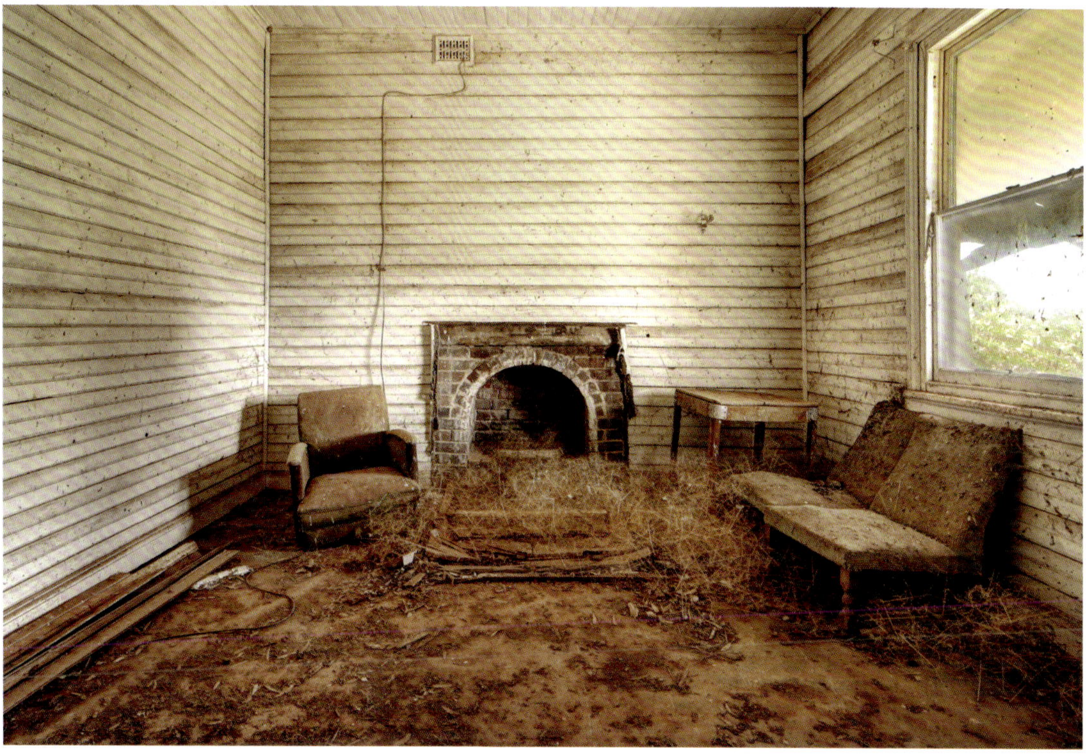

A lounge room with vintage furnishings

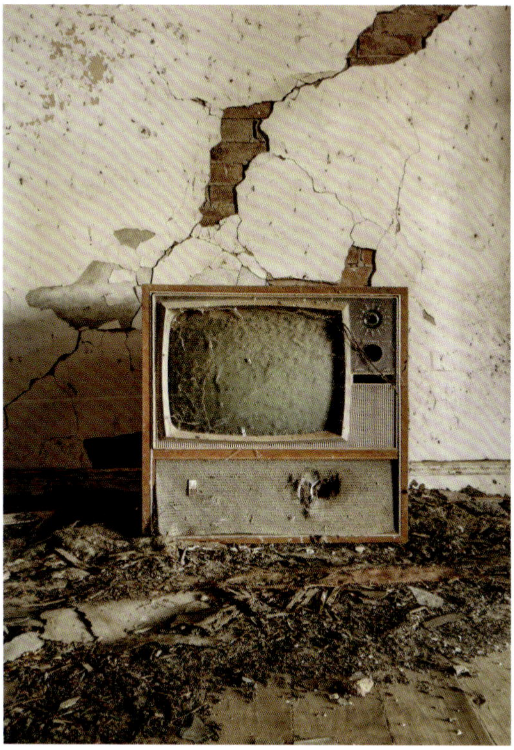

Vintage TV sets are a common feature inside many abandoned farmhouses

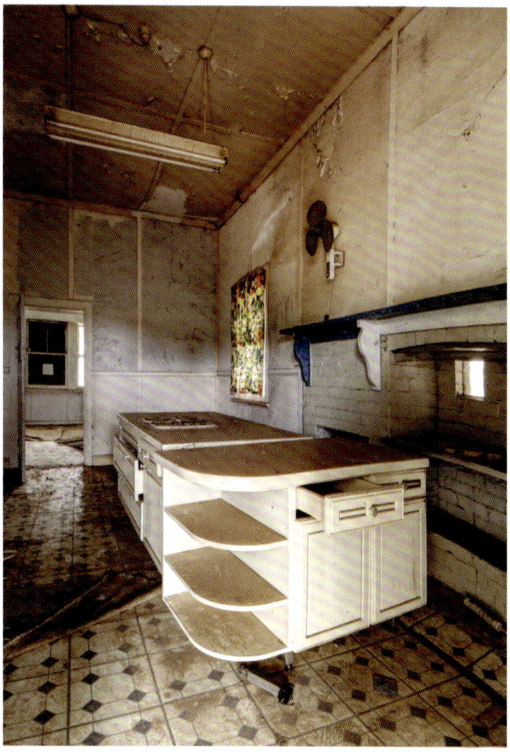

A kitchen still containing original fittings

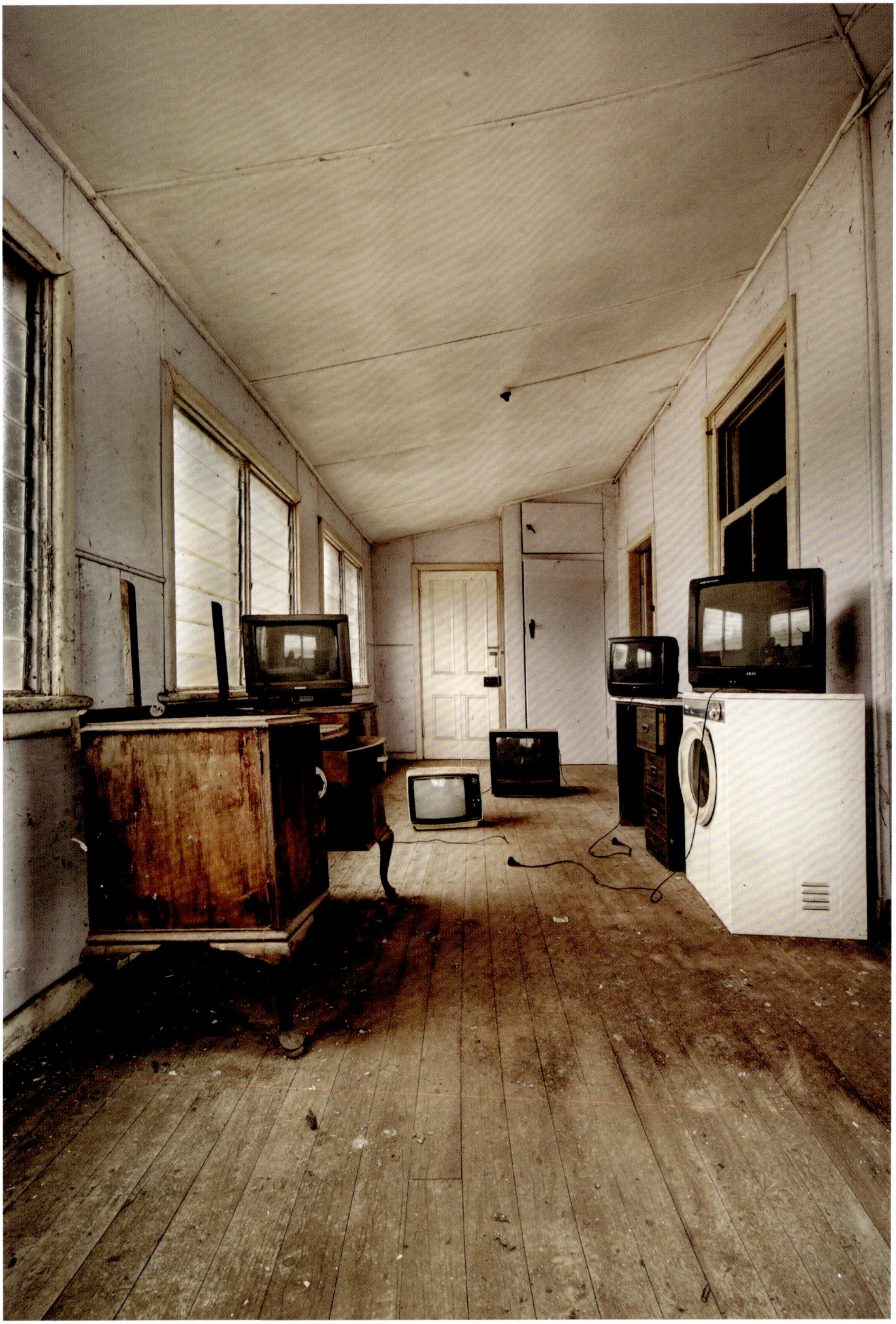

A sunroom contains a number of vintage TV sets

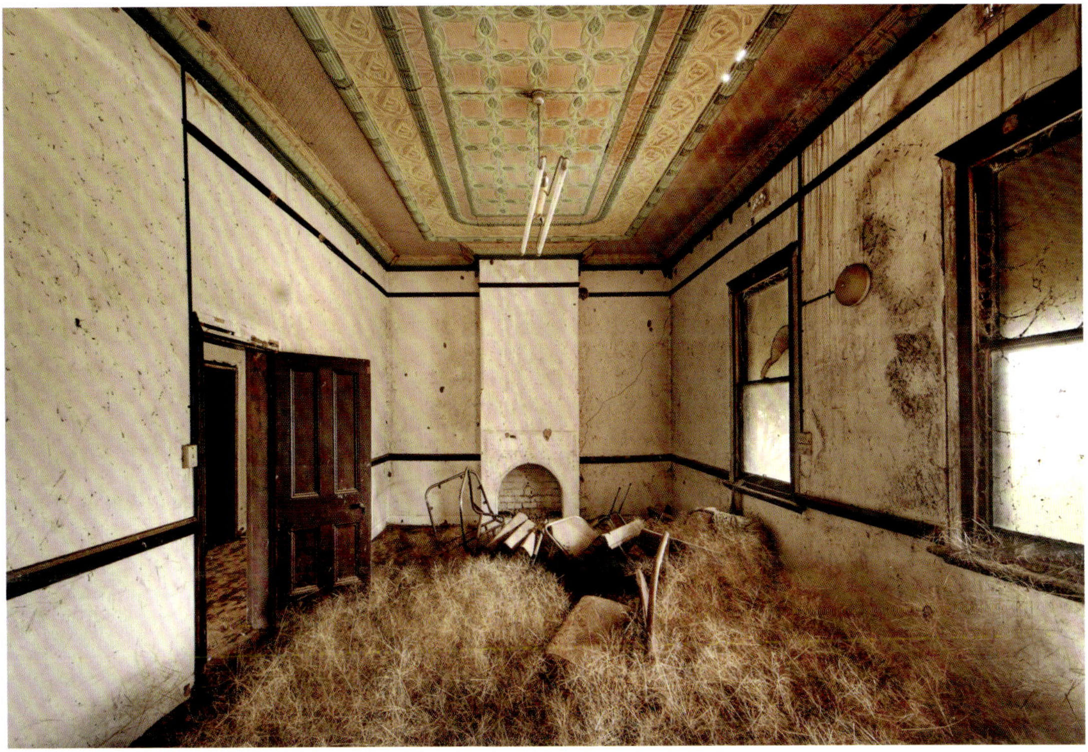

A former dining room, filled with hairy panic

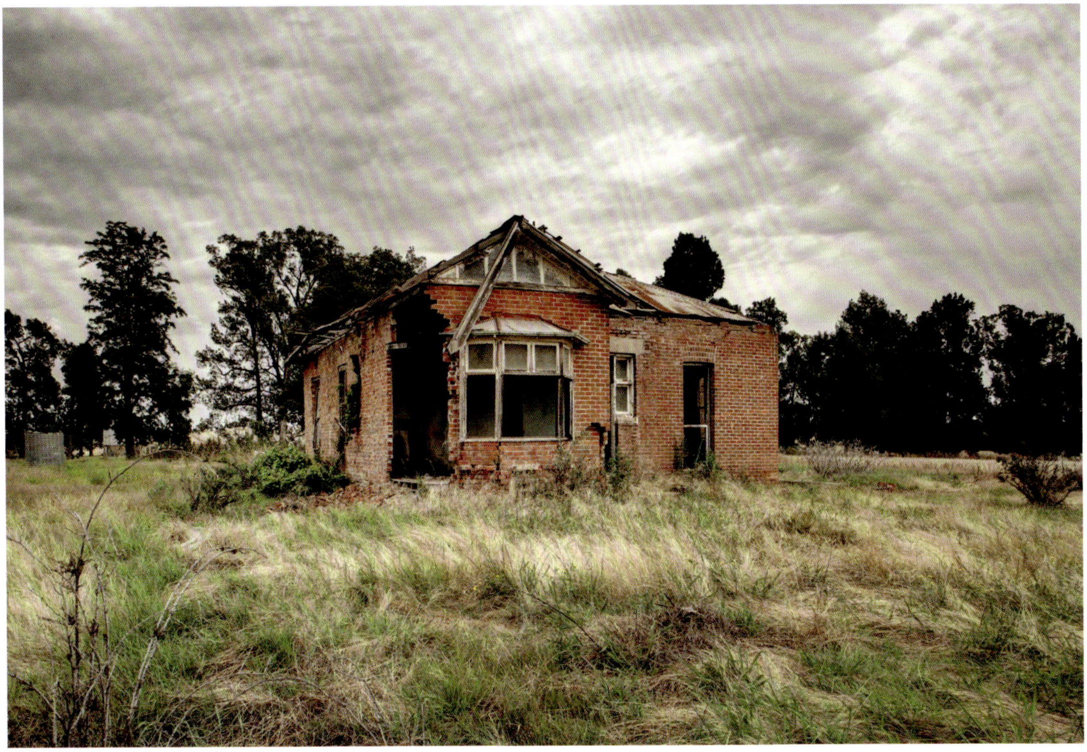

The front facade of a crumbling early 20th century farmhouse

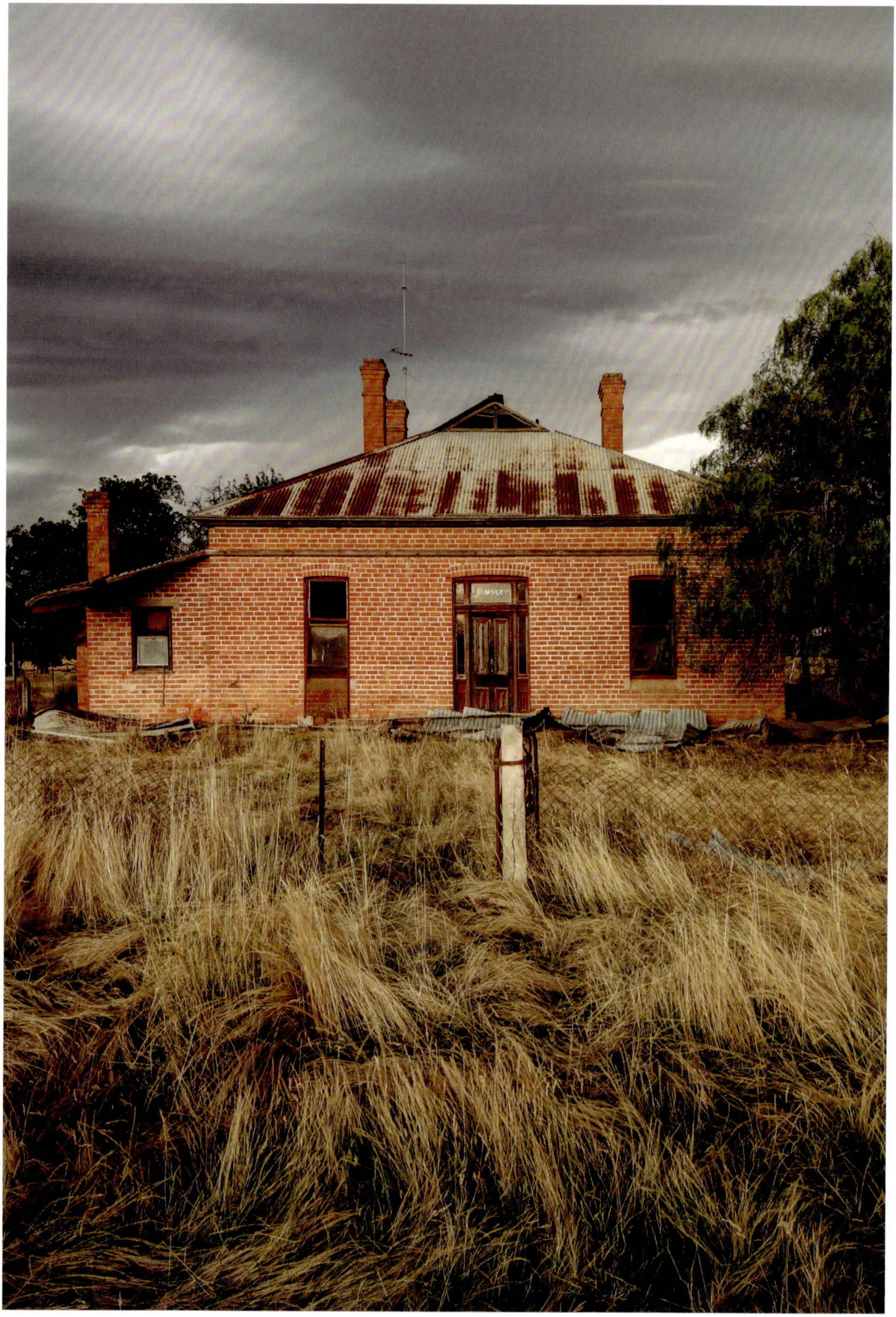

A discarded but furnished homestead sits on a rural property

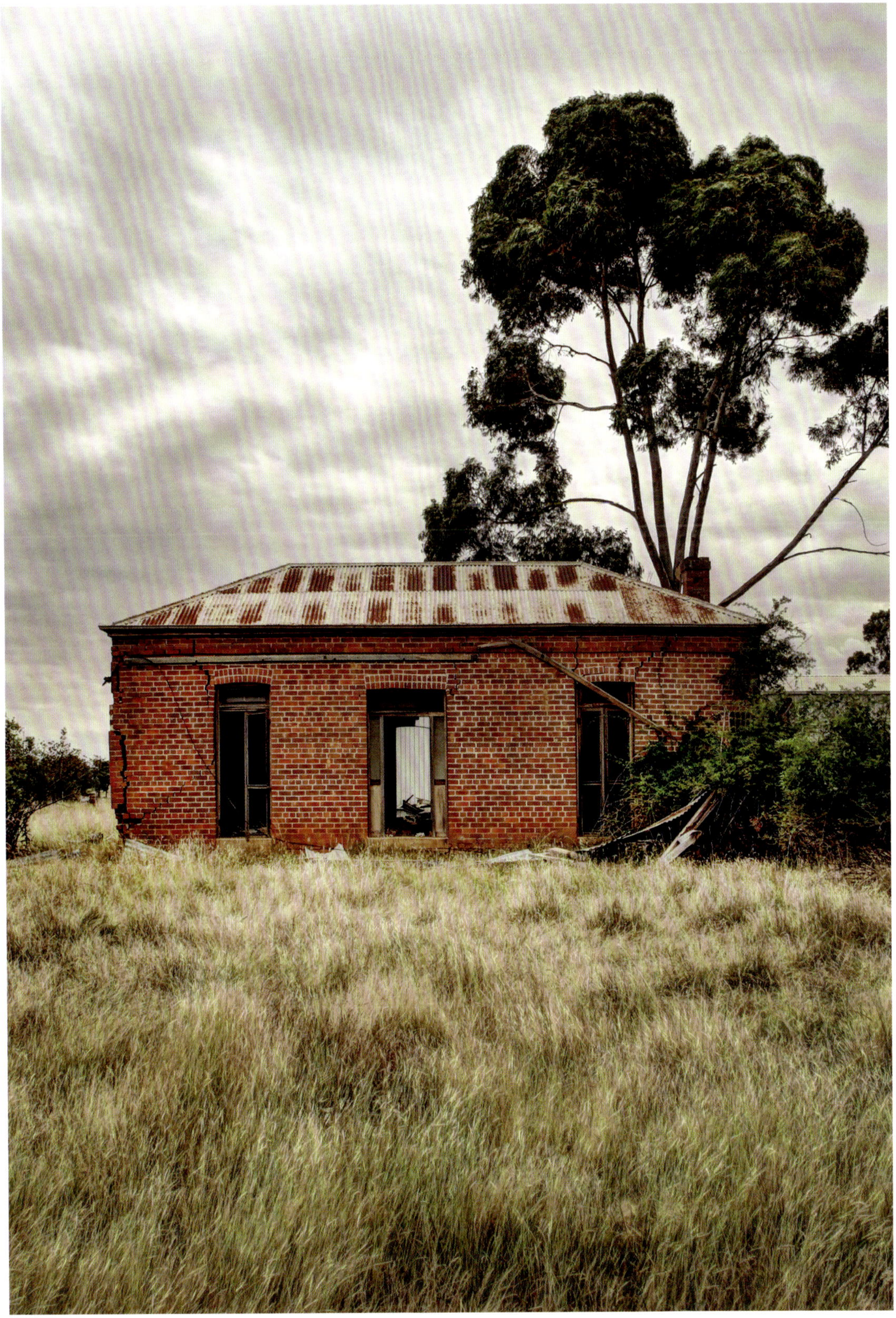

The shell of a former country homestead

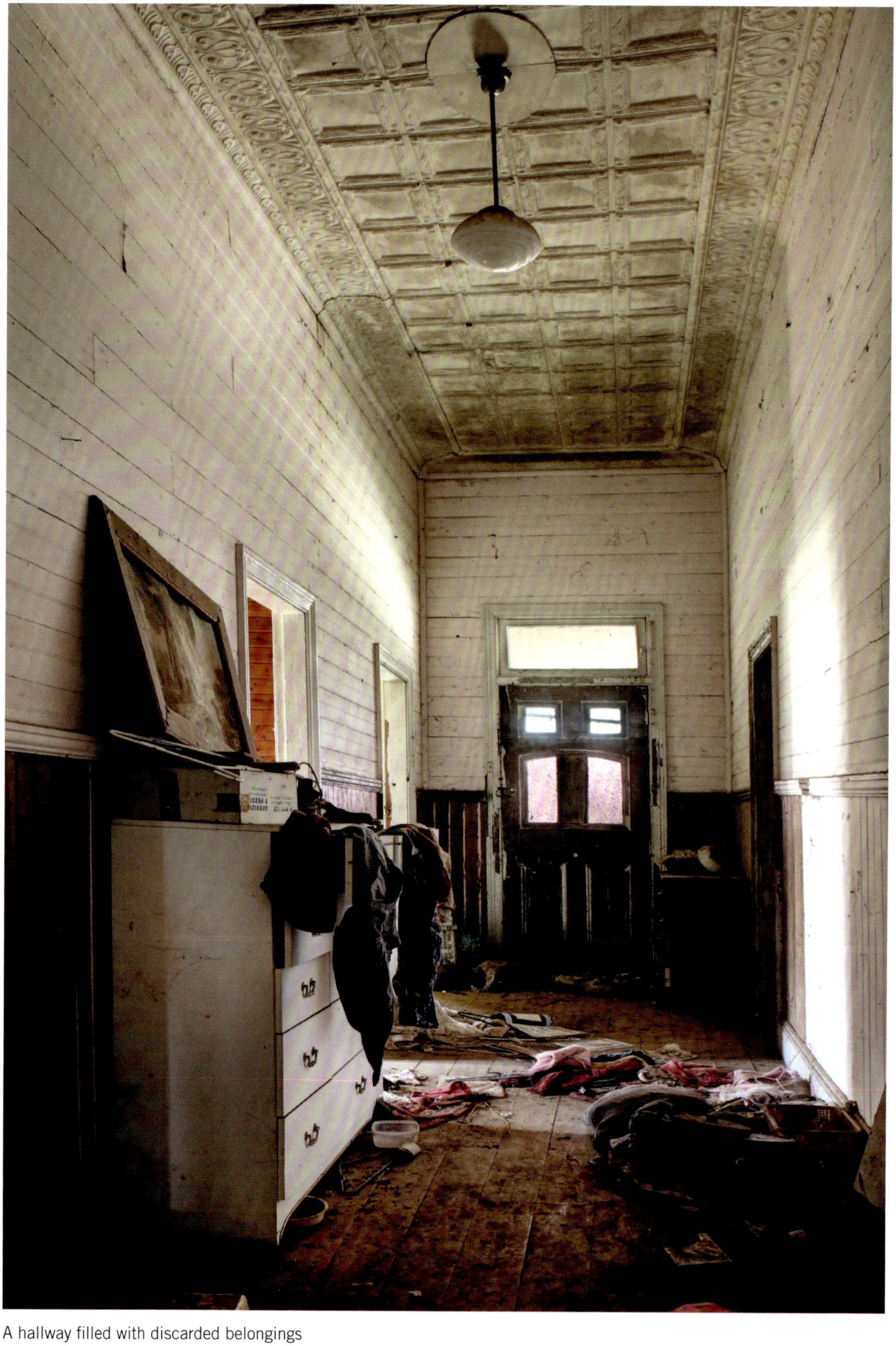

A hallway filled with discarded belongings

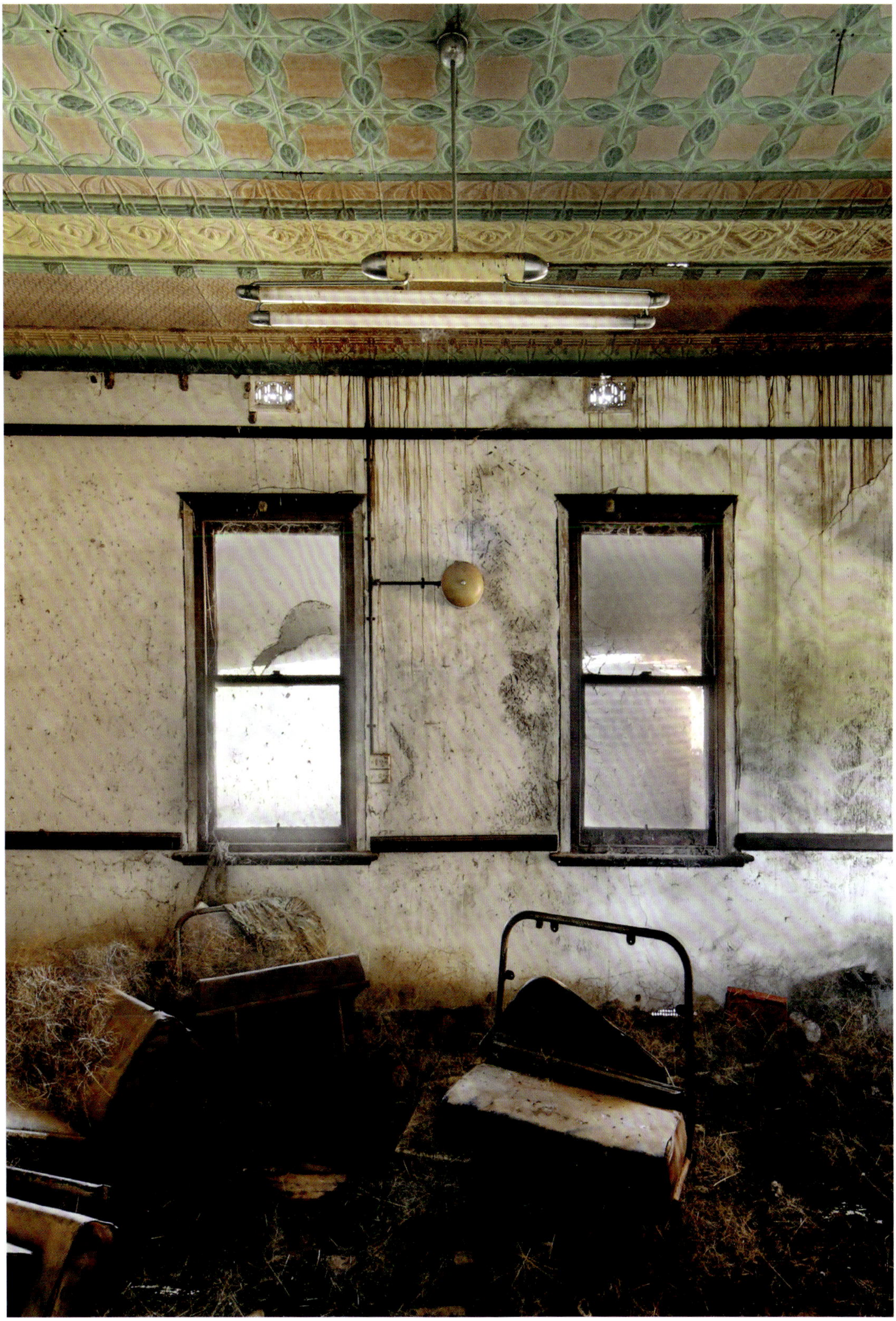

This dining room included an ornate patterned pressed tin ceiling

BOURKE ABATTOIR

Built in the 1940s, this infamous long-abandoned abattoir provided meat to much of the state as well as employment to the local Bourke community. Closing in the 1990s, the now crumbling slaughterhouse still contains the conveyer belts, stock rooms and chillers of more productive days.

Located on the outskirts of Bourke, the area is the traditional home of the Ngemba people. Rusted and dilapidated on a lonely roadside, the former meat-works bakes in the hot sun with no plans in place for re-development.

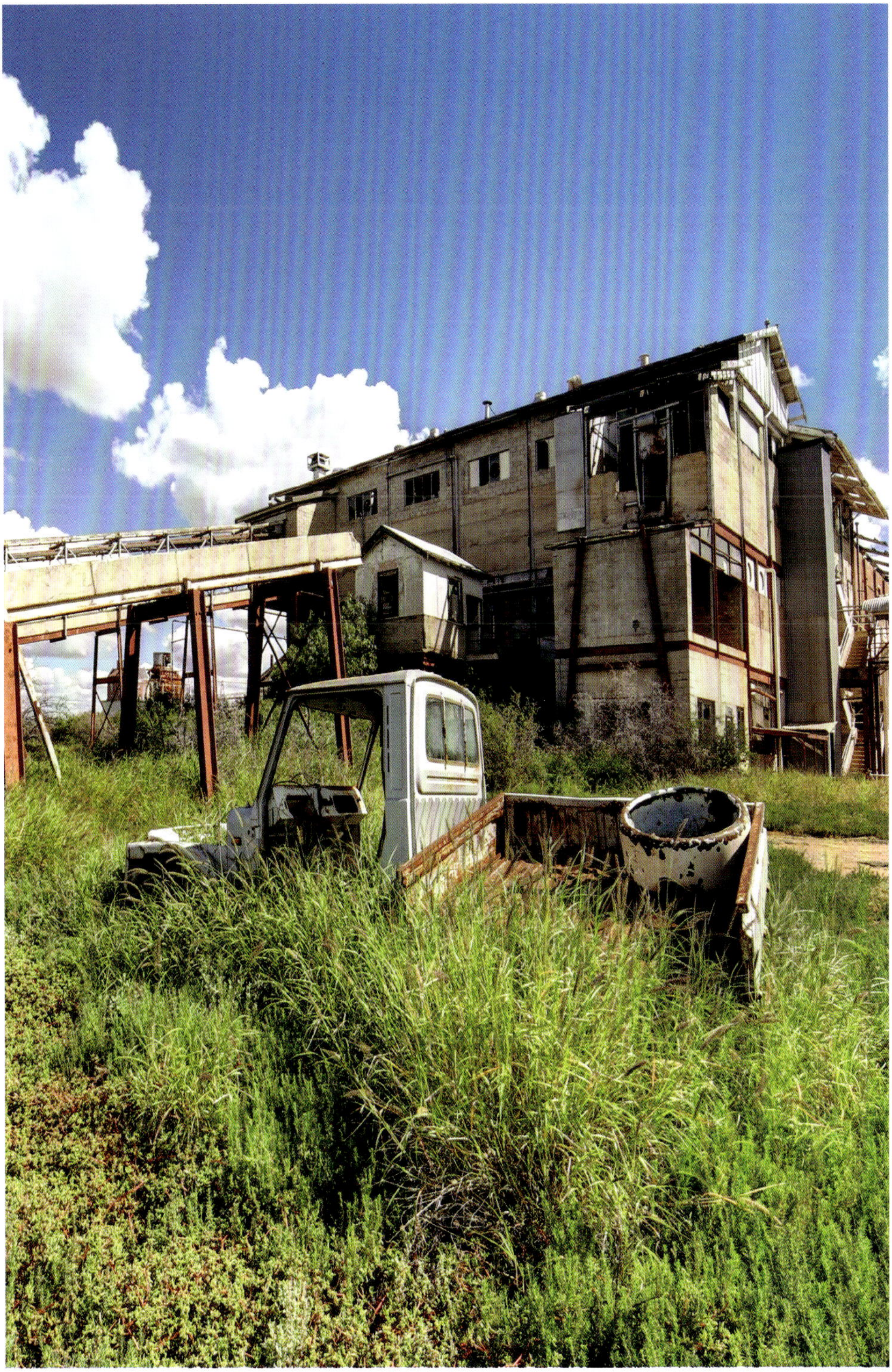

A work truck covered in weeds sits out the front of the abattoir

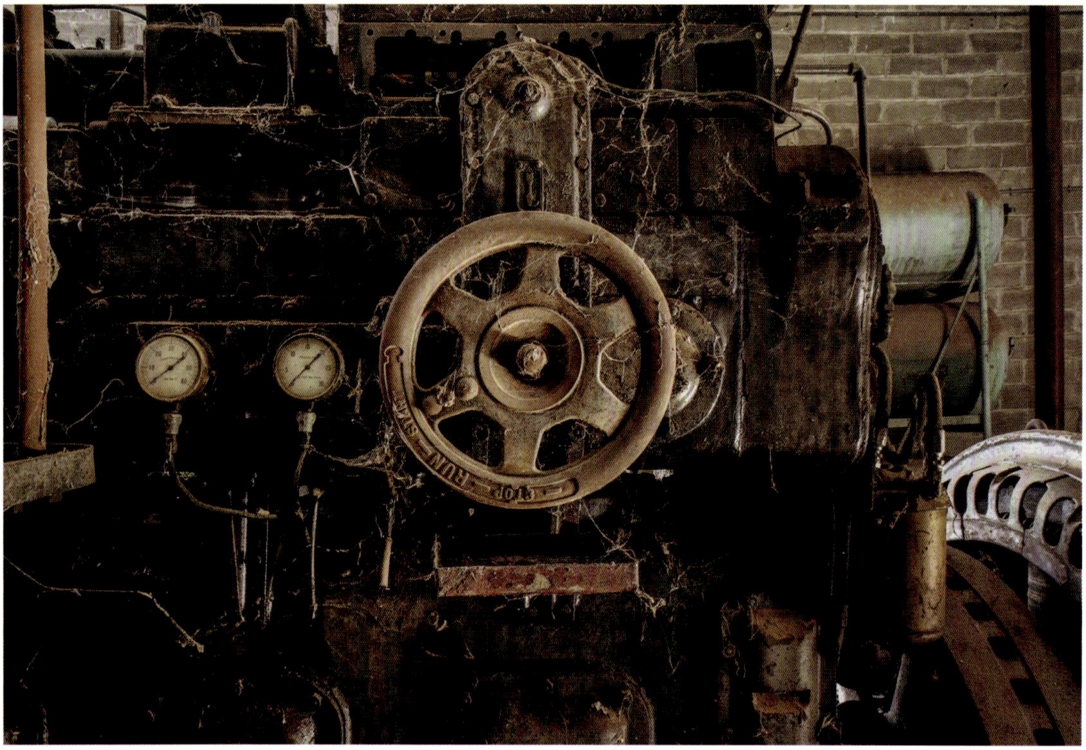

Years of no use have rendered the abattoir's machinery useless

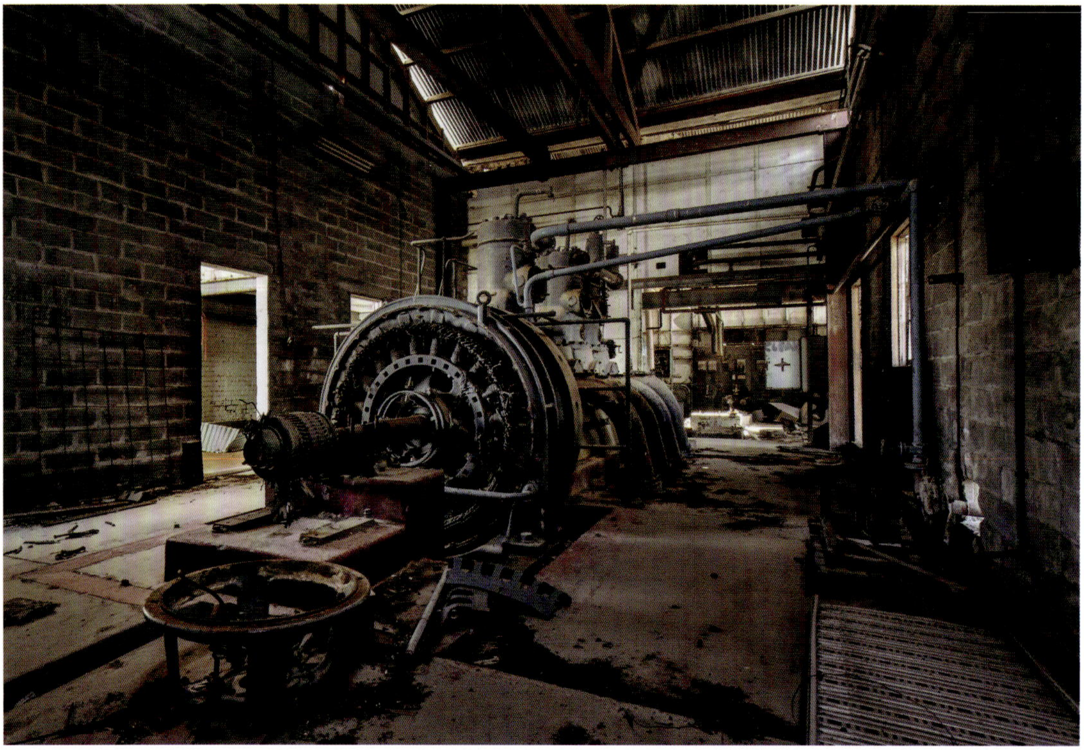

Large machinery in the lower section of the facility

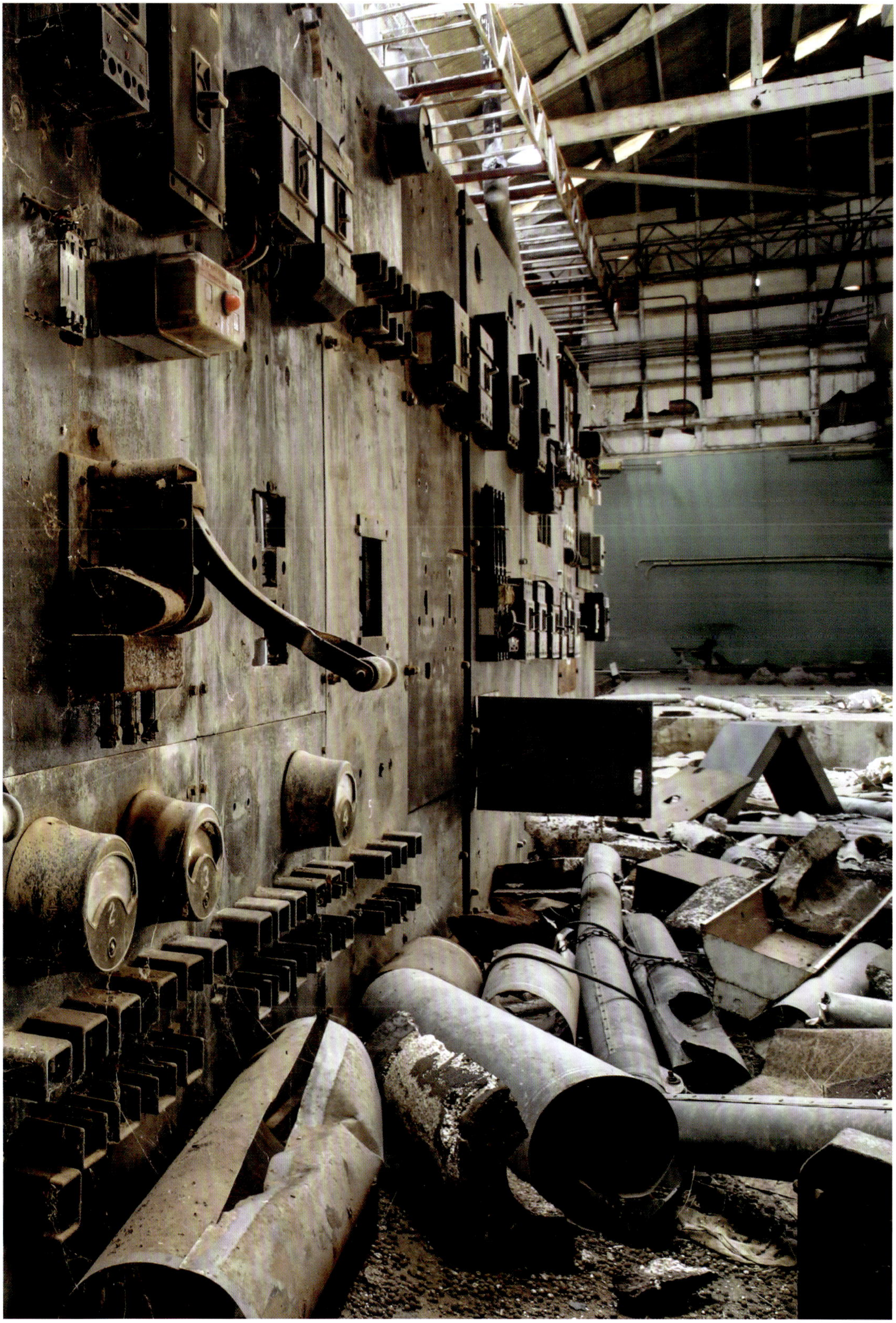
A control panel in one of the abattoir's machine rooms

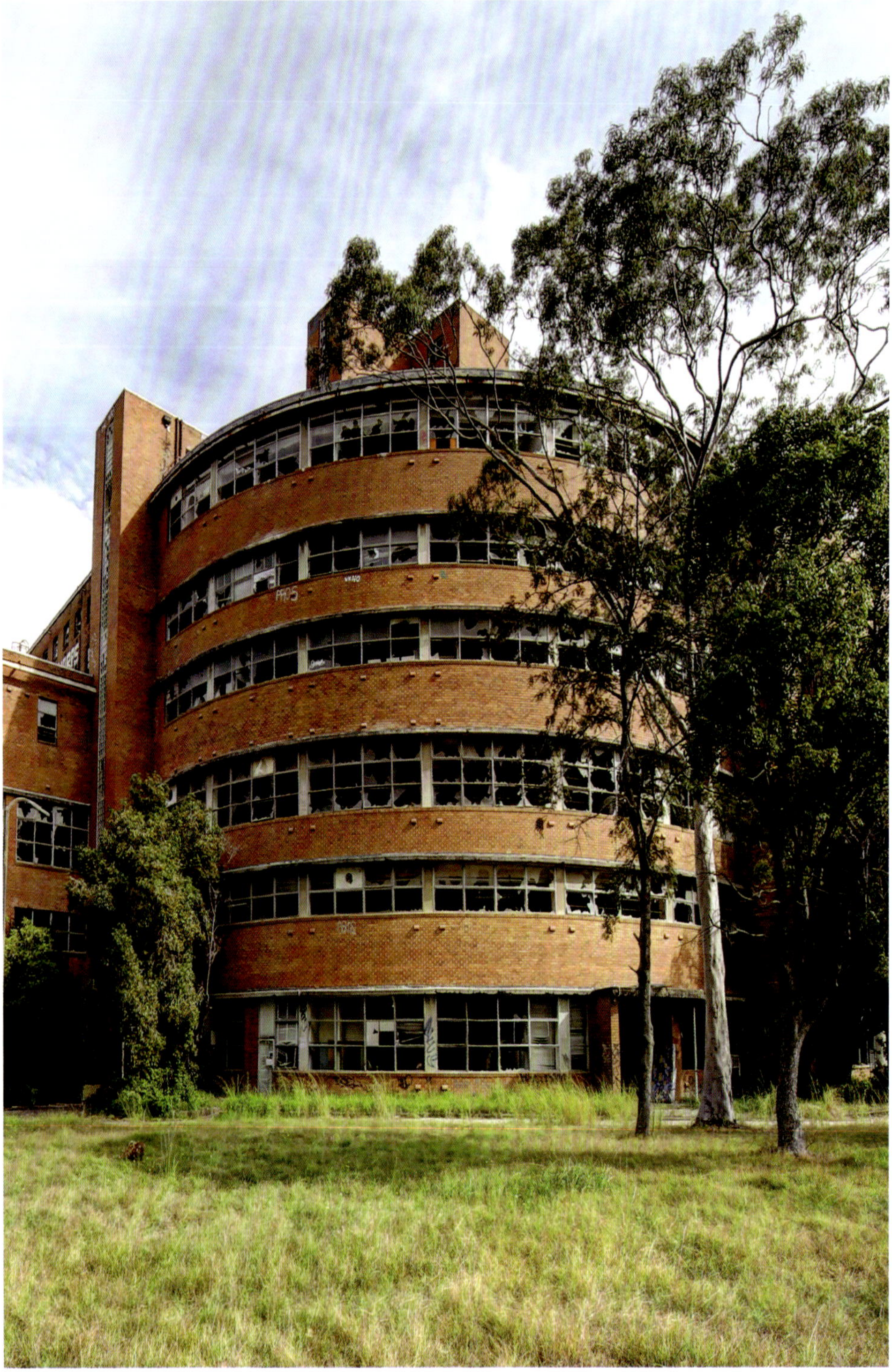

The plant's front façade

THE POWER STATION

The construction of this multi-storey steel and brick building began in the 1950s. Playing a large role in the relief of power shortages across New South Wales, the plant provided much-needed employment to members of the local community. However exorbitant running costs, combined with the introduction of modernised providers ended the facility's life in 1989.

The plant is a valuable slice of the state's heritage, not only due to its vast riveted steel frame, but also because of the 'Fast Tracking' method of construction that was adopted throughout its complex building process. This involved one end of the structure being in production before the other side was fully complete.

A stairwell at the front entrance reaches the facility's upper levels where discarded workspaces are littered with piles of rusted machine parts. Office spaces include desks and cupboards strewn over dusty floors.

In the laboratory, pillaged glass cabinets hang loosely from walls, and ceiling fans dangle on cords, swaying from the wind blowing through the broken windows. Damaged porcelain basins line the worker's washrooms and storage lockers lay across linoleum floors in darkened change rooms. Stepping into the facility's main building provides an appreciation of the power plant's gargantuan size, with its vast engine room stretching off into the distance.

Today, the space remains abandoned. With frequent occurrences of vandalism and an uncertain future, this crumbling megastructure is currently searching for a developer to transform the 60,000-square metre area into a functioning urban zone.

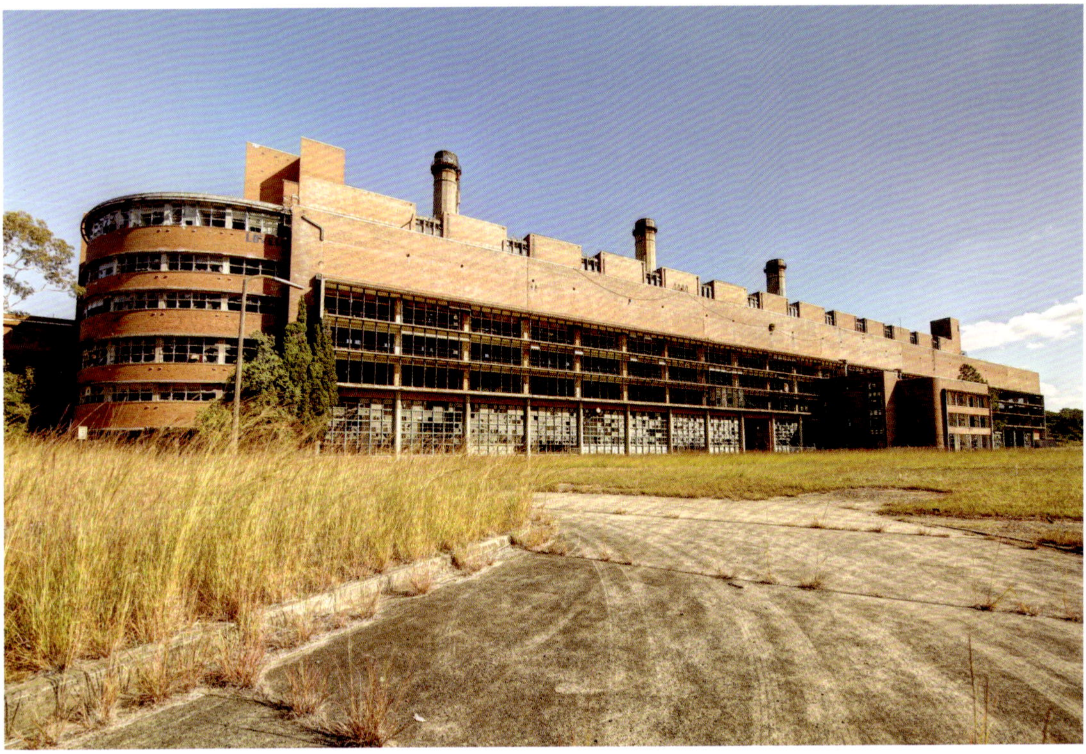

This long view shows the gargantuan size of the structure

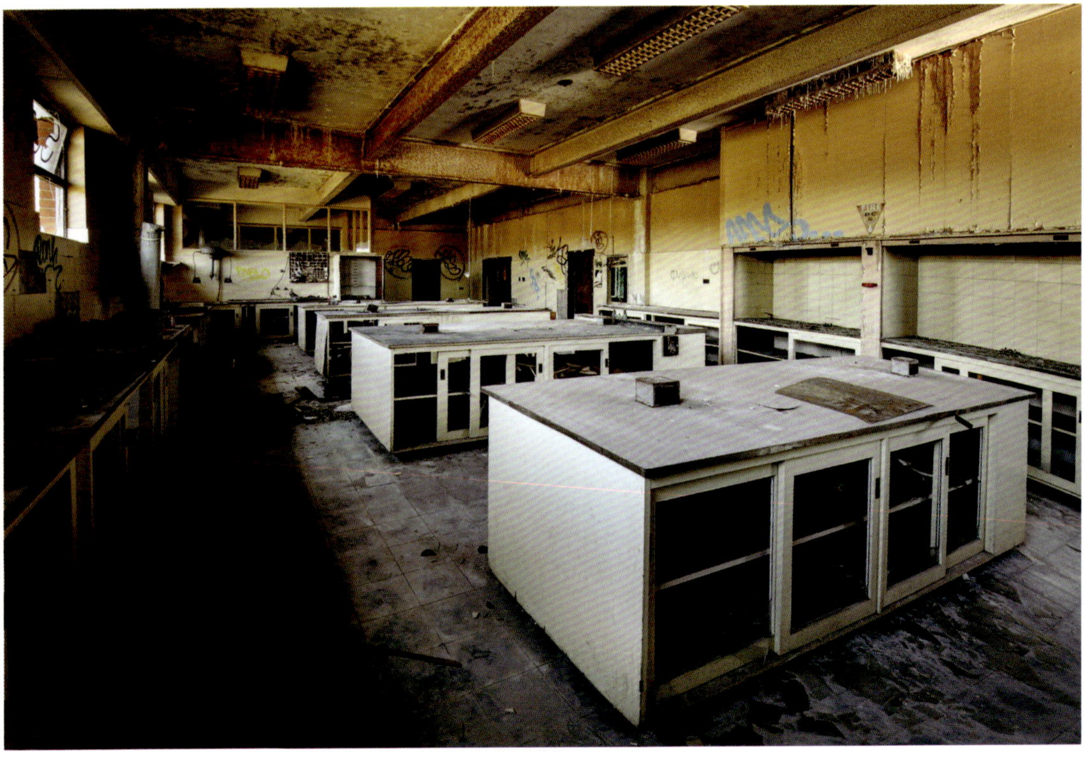

A former laboratory space lined with work benches

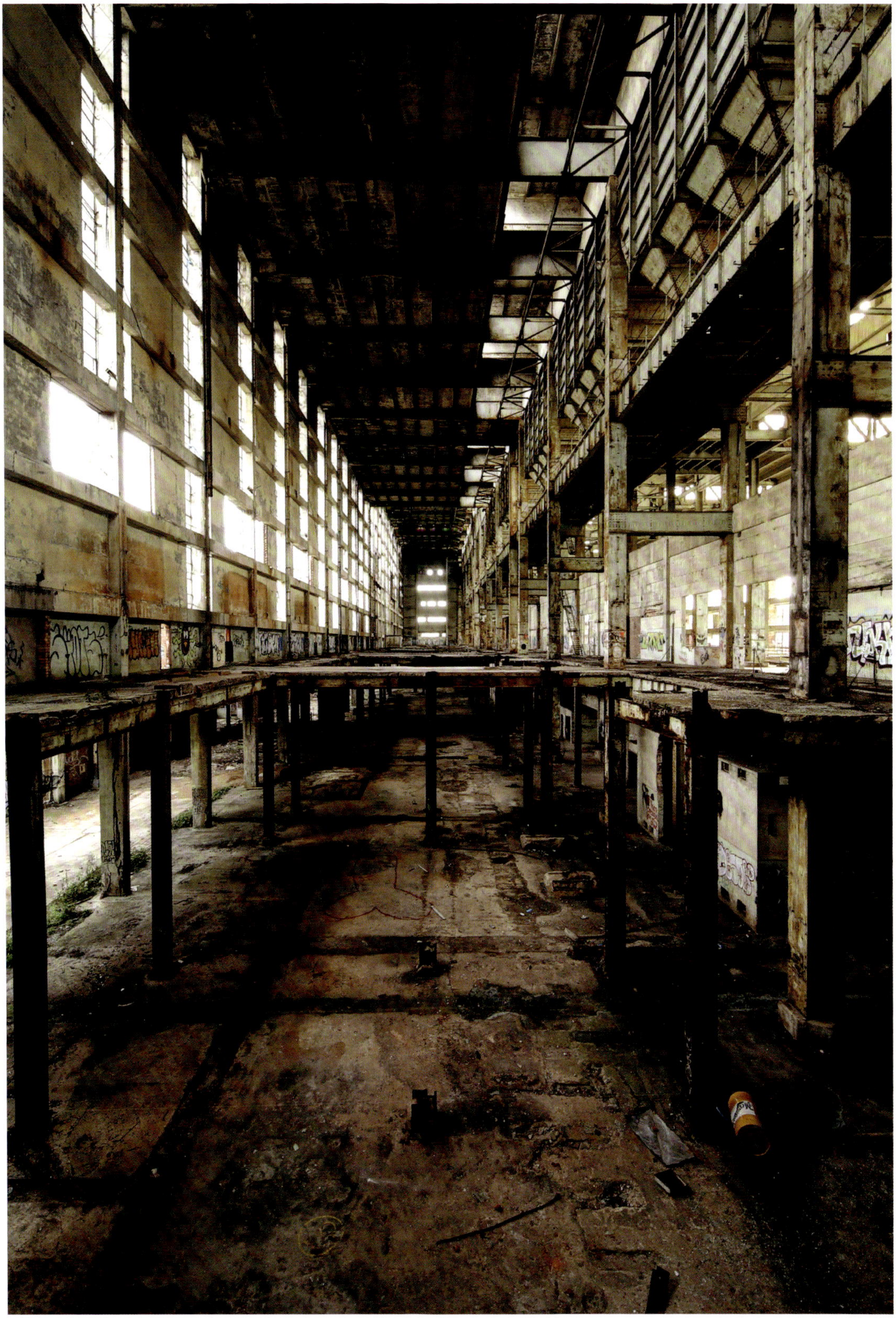

An interior view of the vast engine room; its inner mechanics have been removed

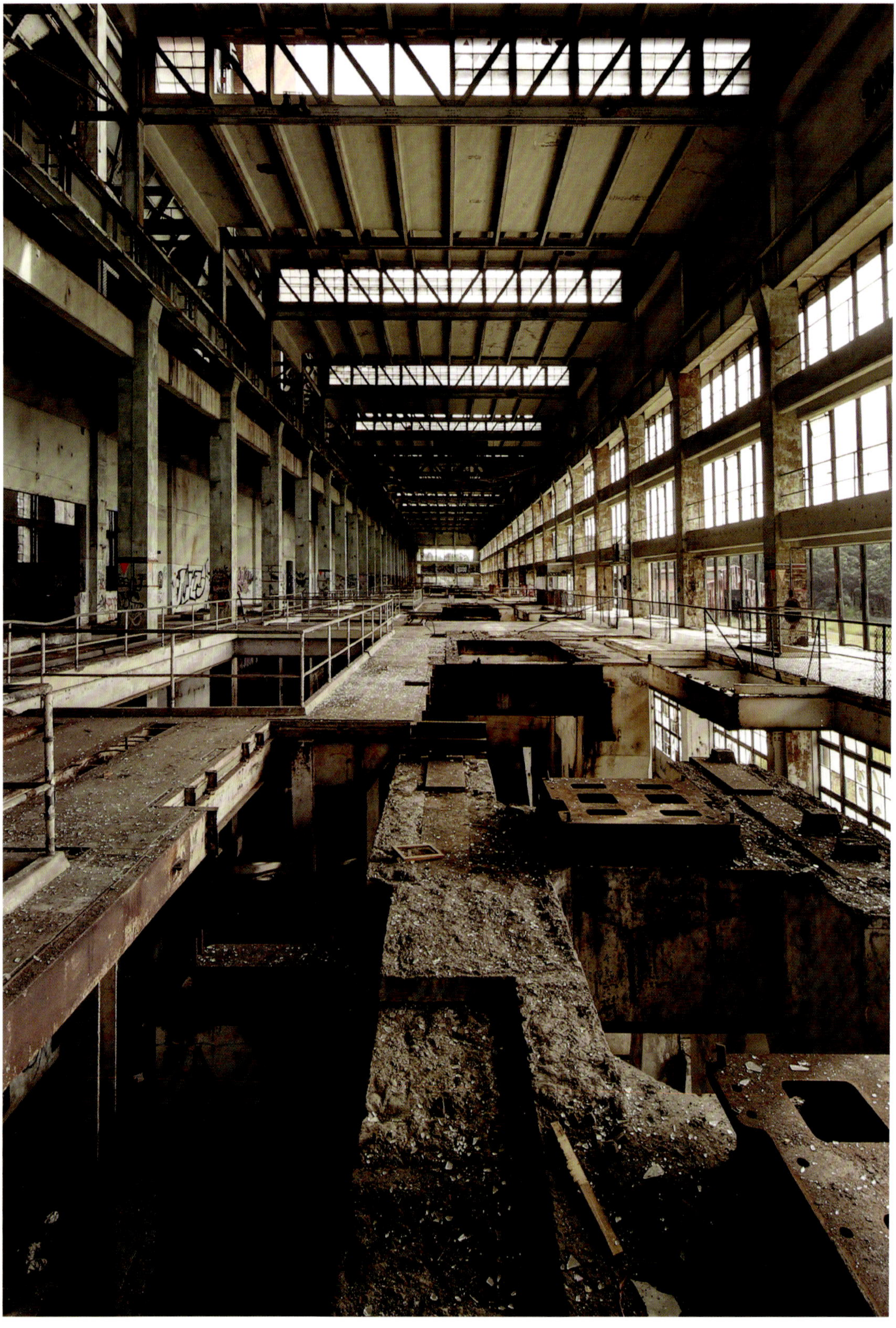

Long view of a rust-covered engine room

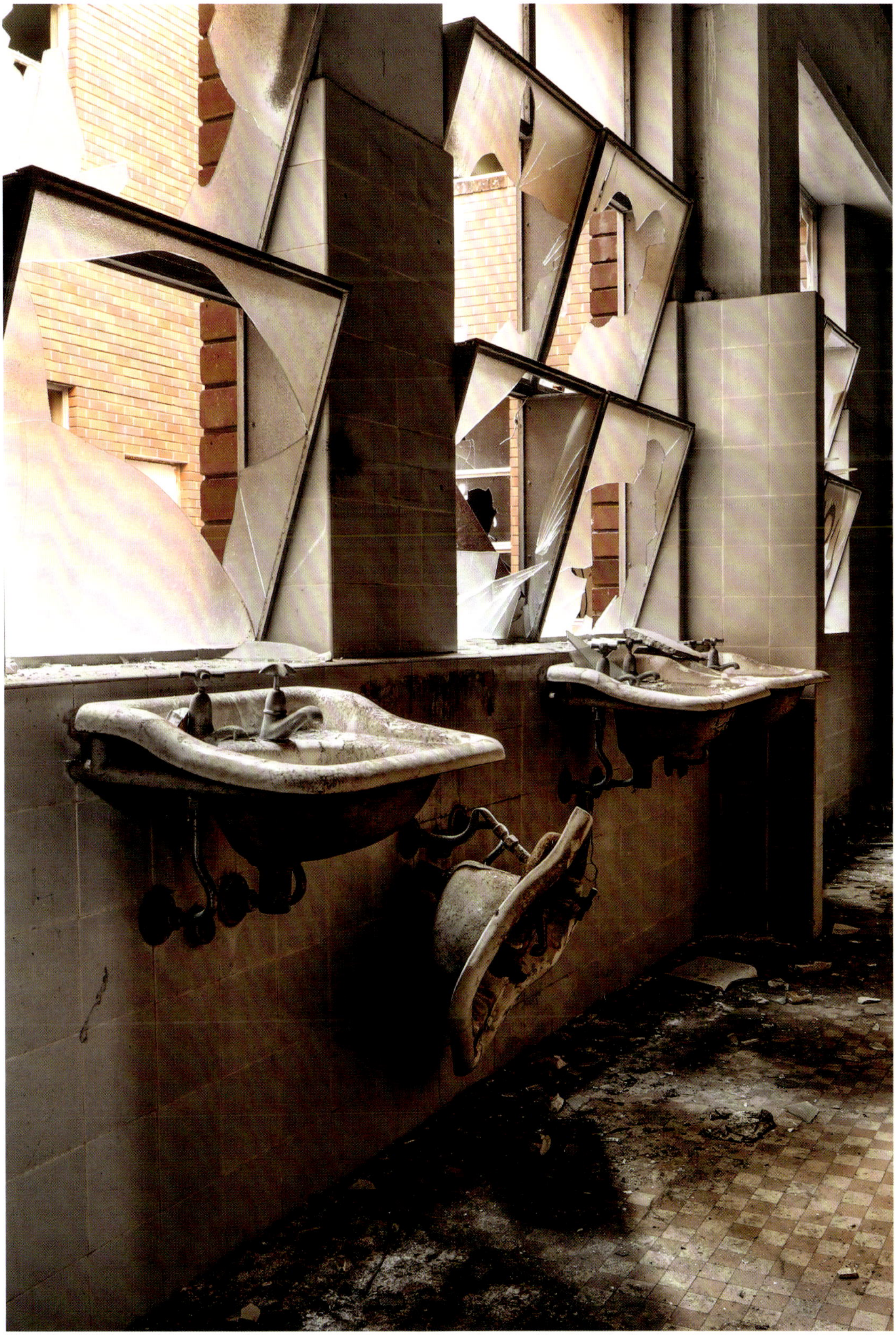
Smashed basins inside a heavily vandalised washroom

GLEN DAVIS

The remnants of the former Glen Davis mine lay scattered amongst trees and nature in the picturesque Capertee Valley. Mining operations commenced in the 1940s, employing approximately 170 workers during the Great Depression. Providing much-needed oil for the defence forces, a cessation in government funding combined with resource depletion in the 1950s resulted in the permanent closure of the facility.

Trees, vines and shrubs engulf several broken structures now home to a range of native birds. Mobs of kangaroos run rife throughout the area, leaping between the abandoned cars that lay both in and around scattered mounds of bricks and ruins.

This is a space where the natural and unnatural clash together to create a contrary story where human industrialisation faces the wrath of mother nature. Gigantic sandstone cliffs surround the scene, creating a silent and ghostly enclosure where an ancient landscape consumes a once-prosperous twentieth century mine.

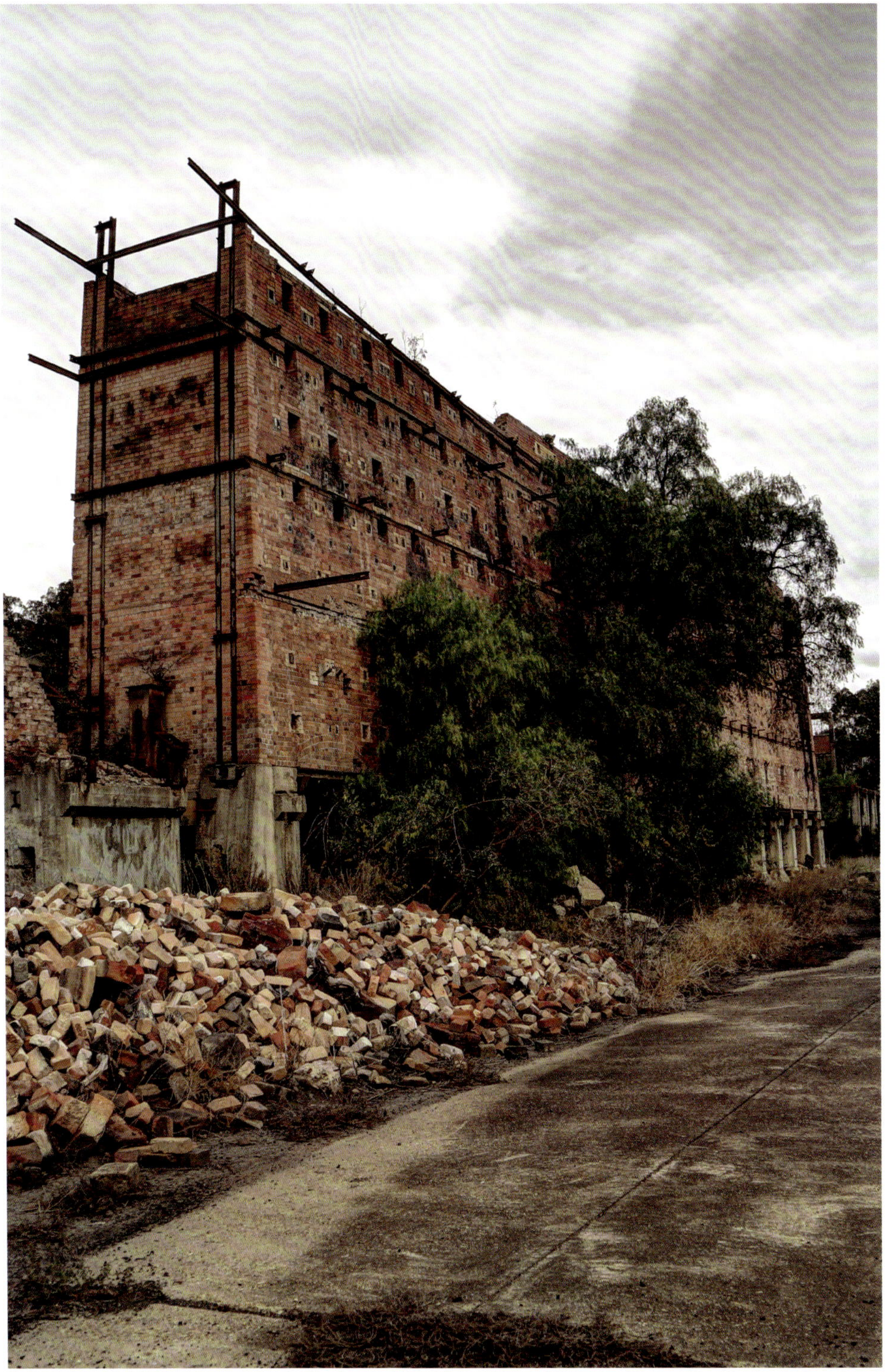

One of Glen Davis' many crumbling structures

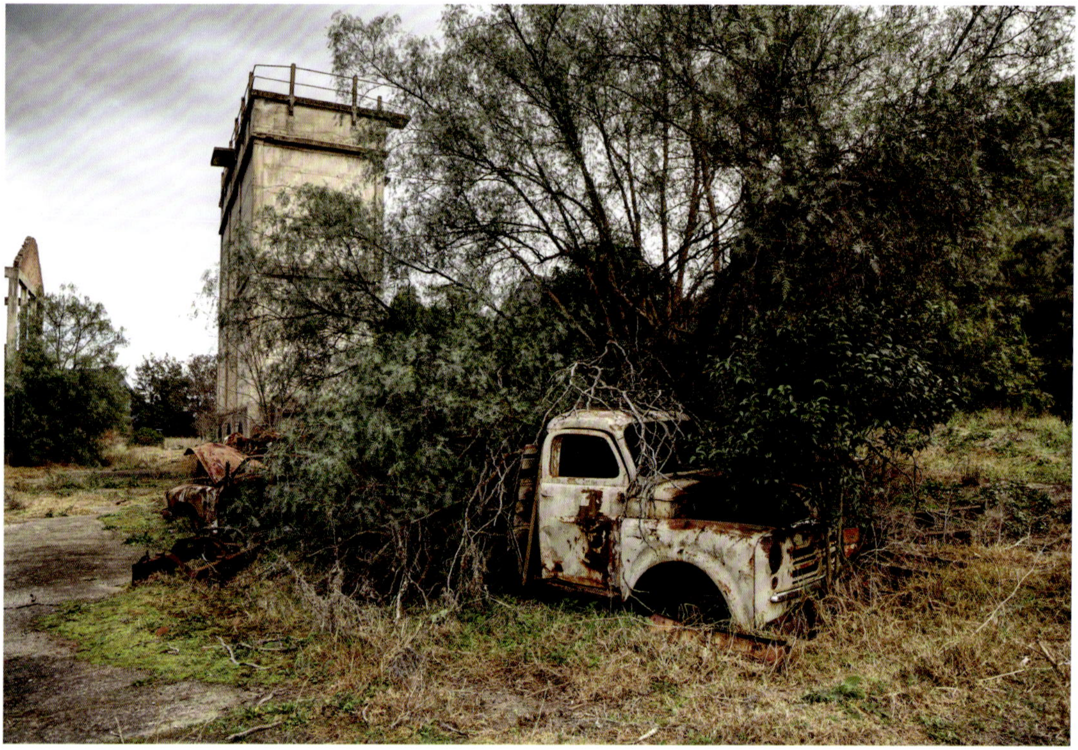

A truck engulfed by trees and shrubbery

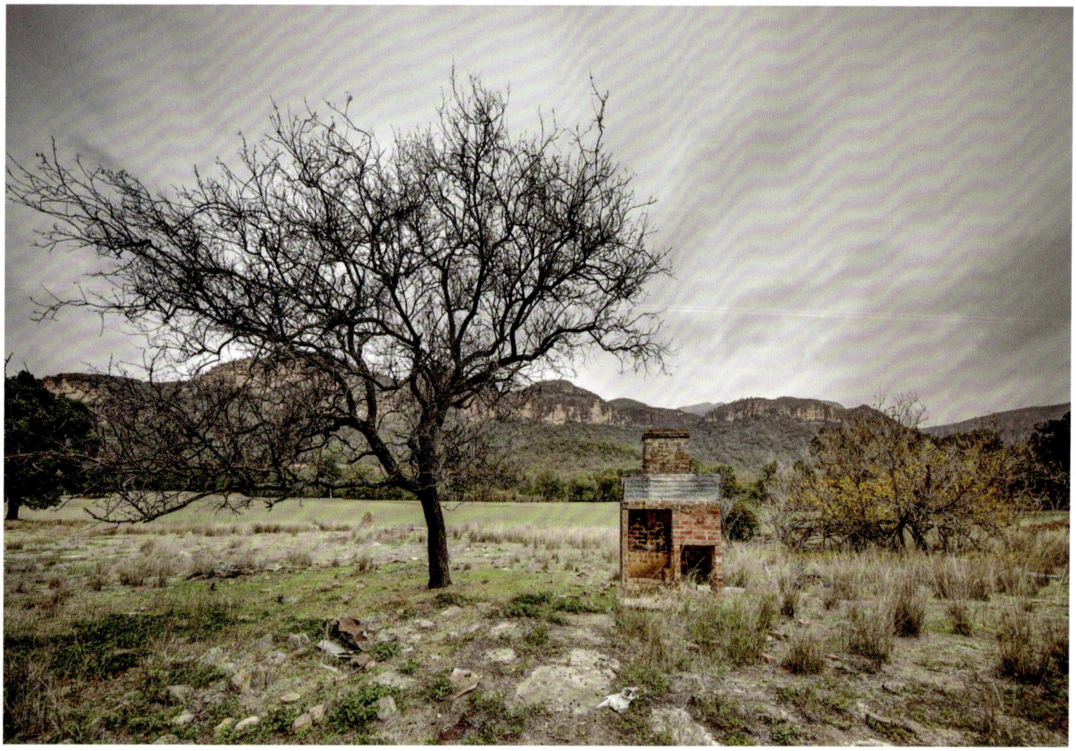

A number of fireplaces are scattered around the area; campers often re-use these as fire pits

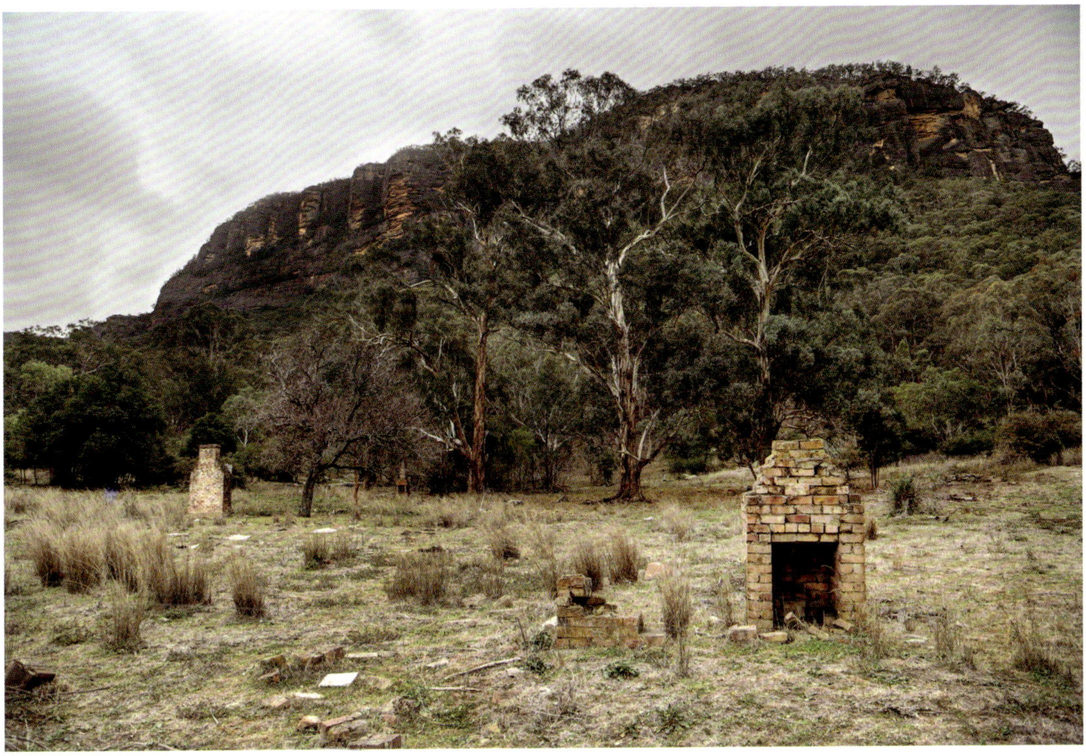

Giant sandstone cliffs provide a picturesque backdrop

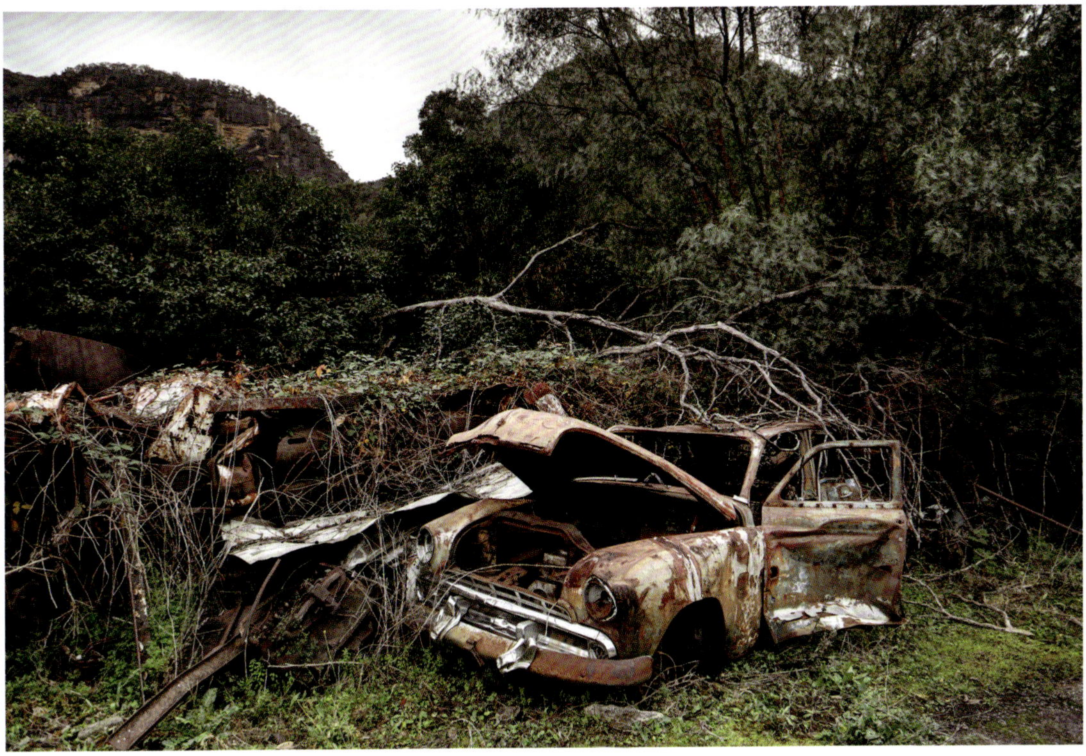

A gap in the shrubs reveals a rusted vehicle

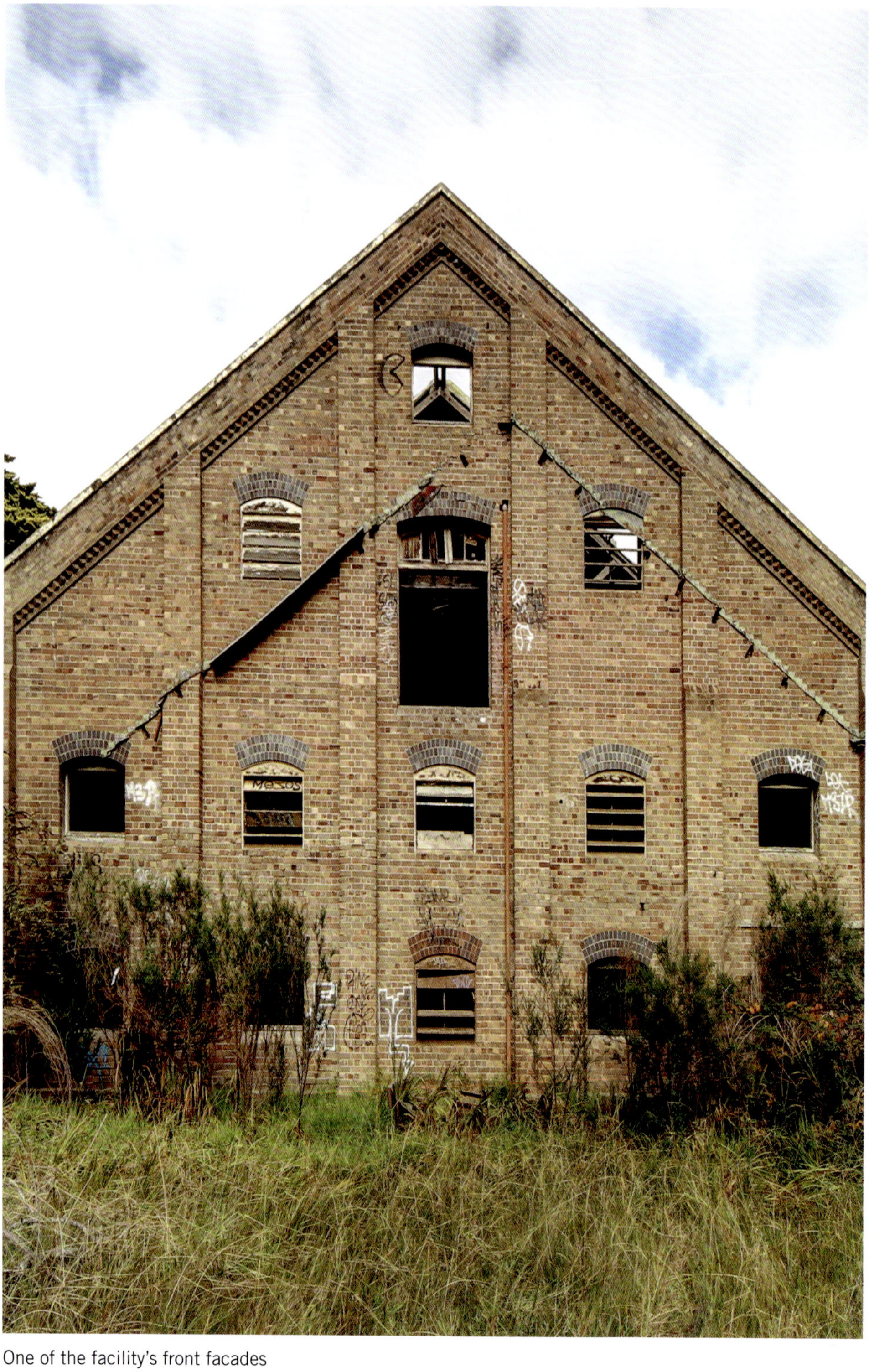

One of the facility's front facades

THE MALTINGS

The bushy Mittagong township provides the scenic backdrop for this discarded early twentieth century malt production plant. Closing permanently in the 1980s, the facility is comprised of three buildings, one of which succumbed to a sizeable blaze in the 1960s.

Positioned in an urban area filled with tree-lined streets and houses, the once accessible space became an unintentional play area for dog walkers, picnic-goers, nature enthusiasts and curious explorers. However, excessive vandalism and several arson attempts forced the grounds' owners to install high-security fencing. This tightly surrounds the dilapidated buildings and the former plant has become an impenetrable fortress with round-the-clock security patrolling the area.

Each structure points to the facility's more industrious days with conveyer belts and rusted machinery remaining inside. In a lower basement, a succession of pillars stretches off into the distance, creating a surreal labyrinthine perspective.

Celebrated historically as cultural monuments that nod to Australia's beer-drinking culture, these dilapidated buildings remind us of the state's more industrious days.

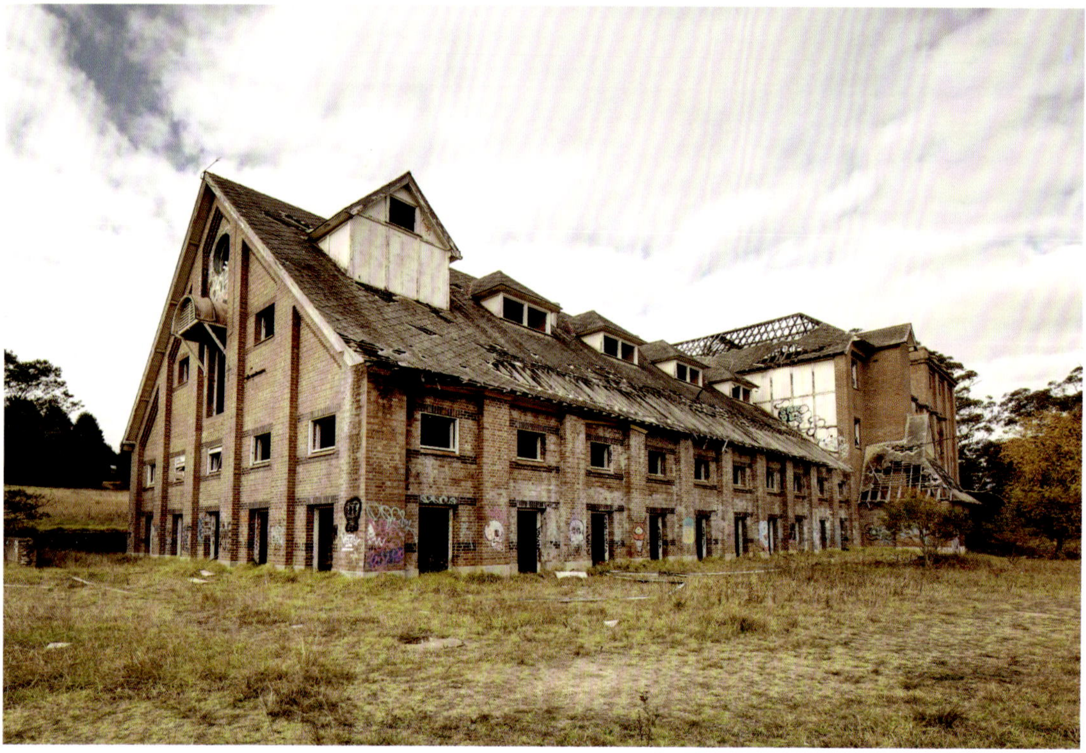

The buildings were constructed in accordance with European architectural principals

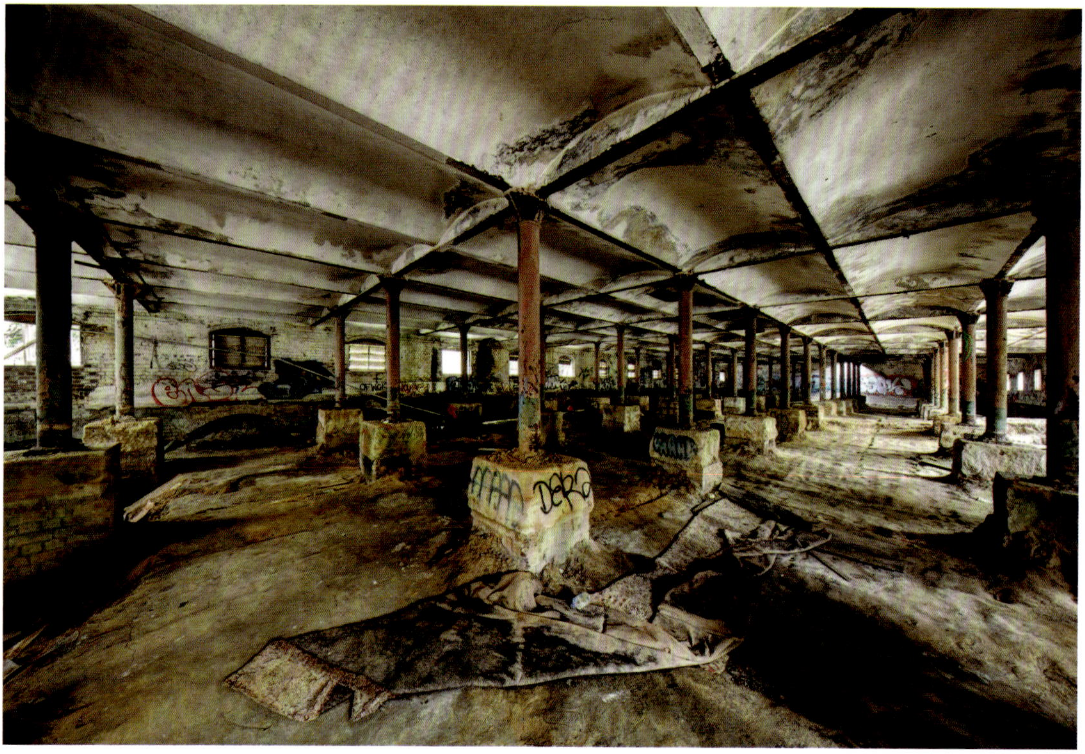

A basement area with a number of pillars stretching off into the distance

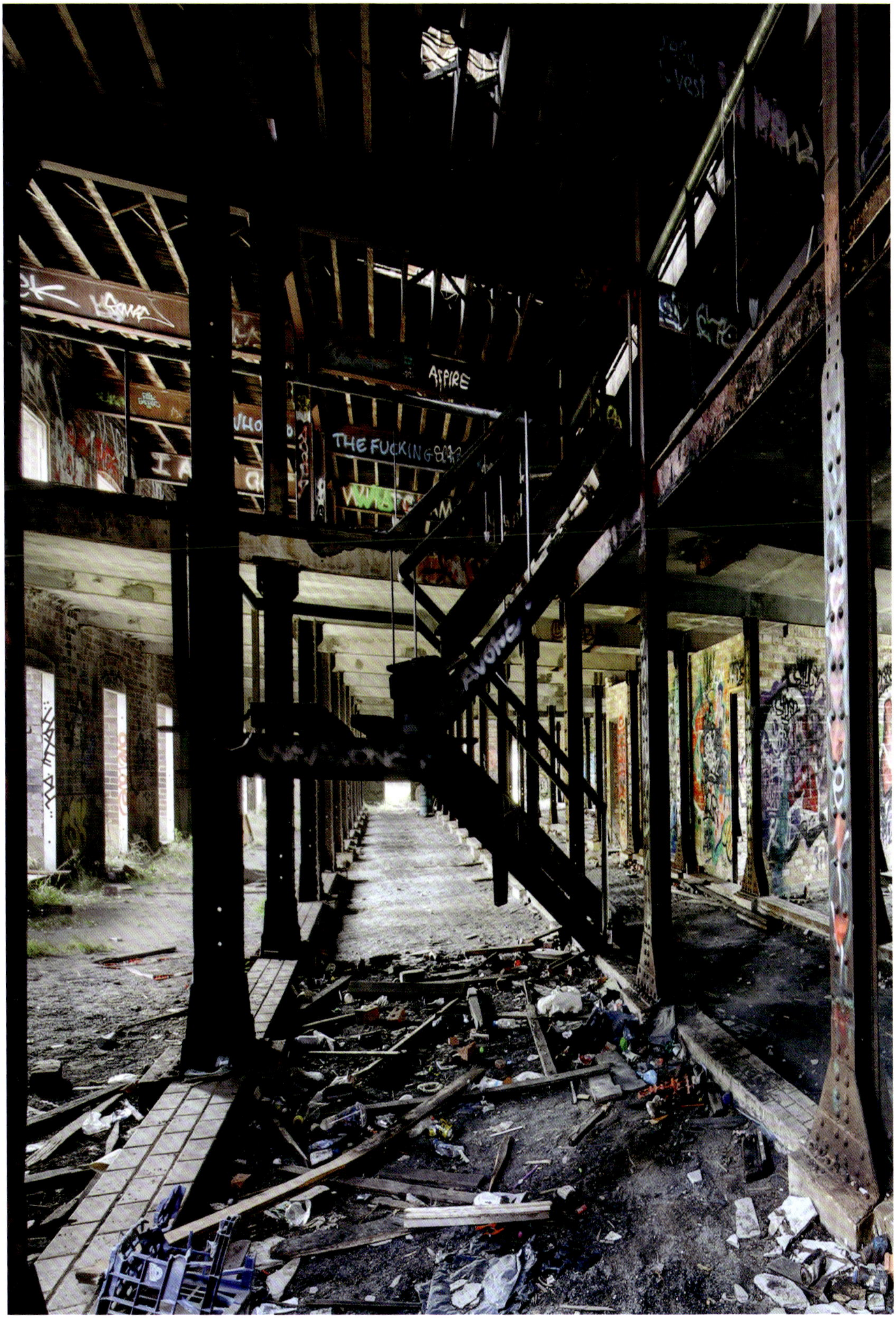

One of the building's heavily vandalised interiors

THE CEMENT FACTORY

Located in the NSW Central Tablelands, the town of Kandos sits beneath Cumber Melon Mountain. Once home to a thriving concrete industry, the area was known as "the place that made the cement that made your town".

Used in bridges, roads, reservoirs, pipes, pathways, fences and buildings, Kandos cement was also poured into the Sydney Harbour Bridge and the city's underground railway. Most famously, its concrete was a significant contribution to the development of the Opera House.

Migrants added much-needed skills and growth to the township, which housed several refugees in the 1950s and 1960s from both European and Middle Eastern backgrounds. Immigration still plays an important role in the town's ongoing cultural story.

Inefficient technology, exorbitant running costs and a shortage of skills resulted in the permanent closure of the factory in 2011. What remains is a dilapidated, industrial palace-like structure tucked away in a valley. With ample spaces to explore, this dust-filled relic is a reminder of more thriving and industrious economic times.

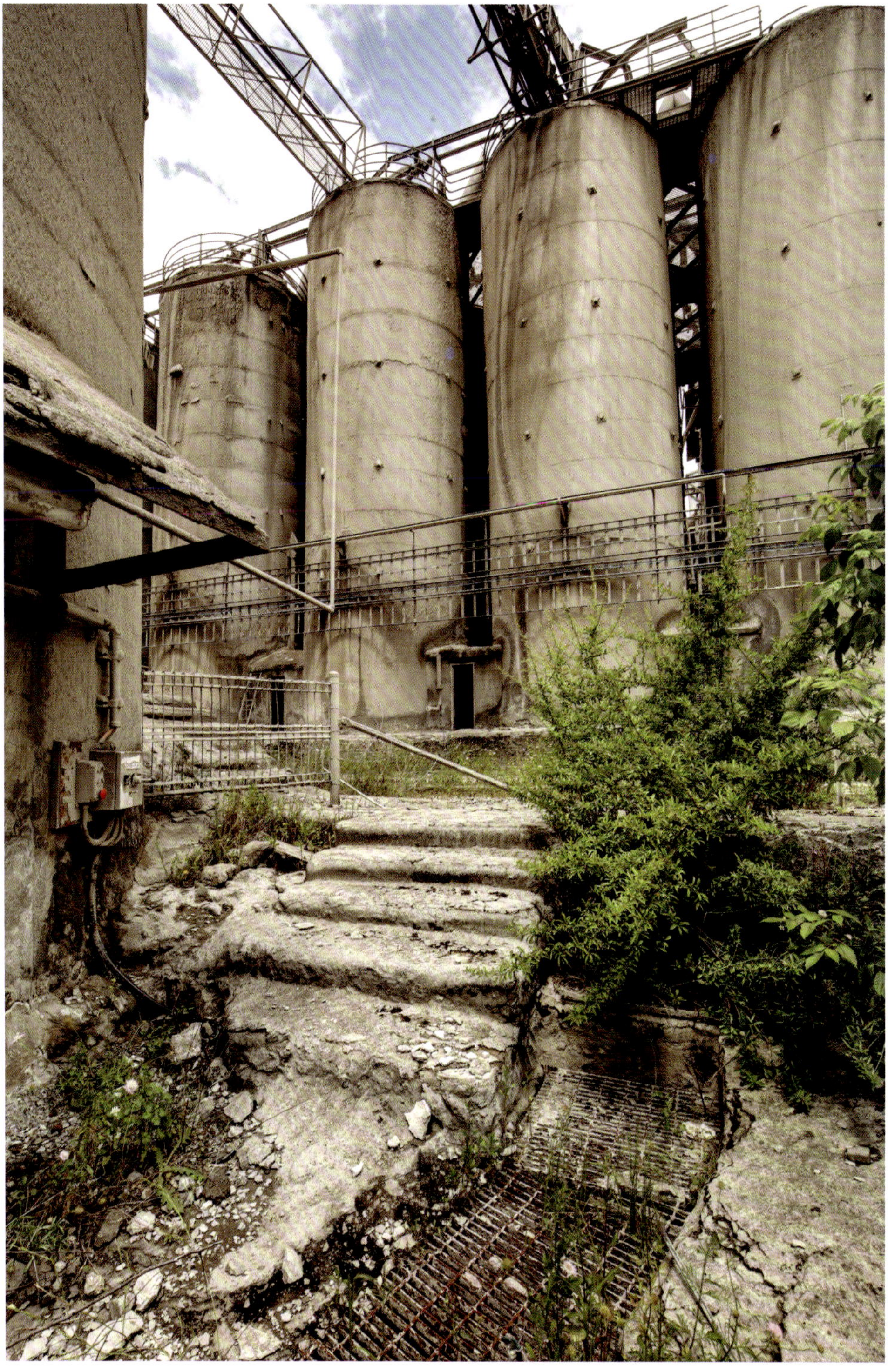
Towering concrete silos cast shadows over the factory's grounds

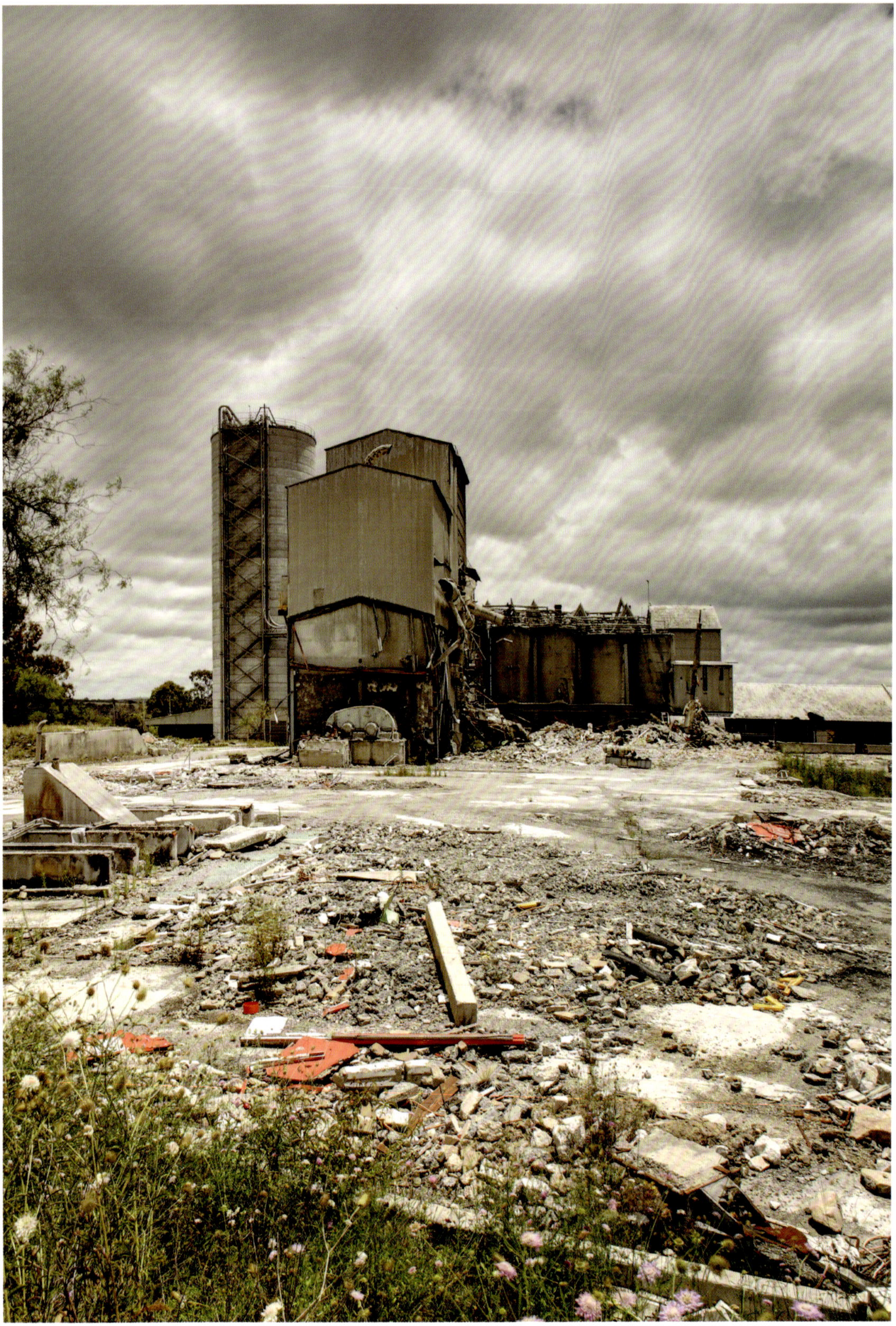

Some viewing points of the facility are reminiscent of a post-apocalyptic war zone

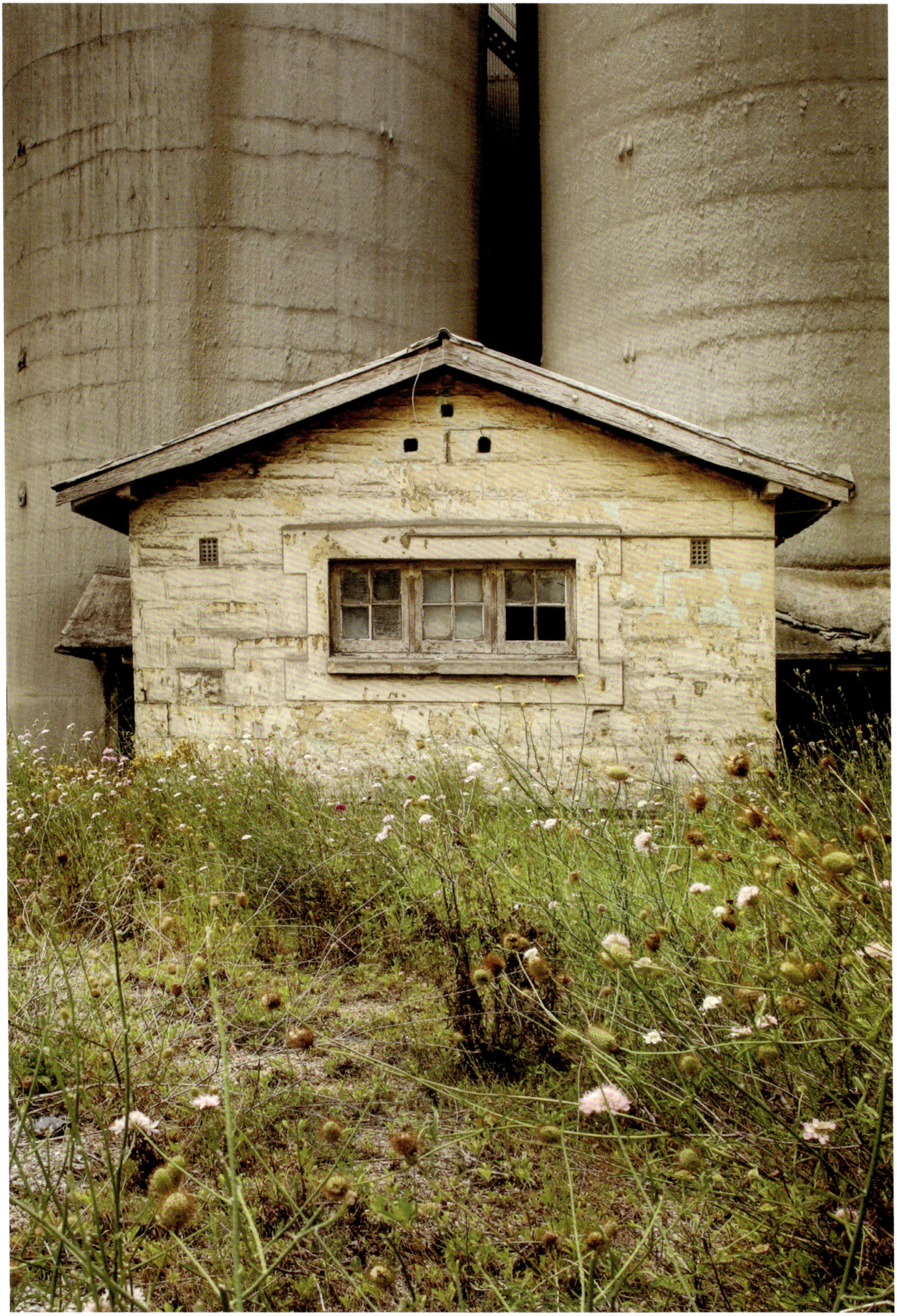

A small storage and office building sits beneath the silos

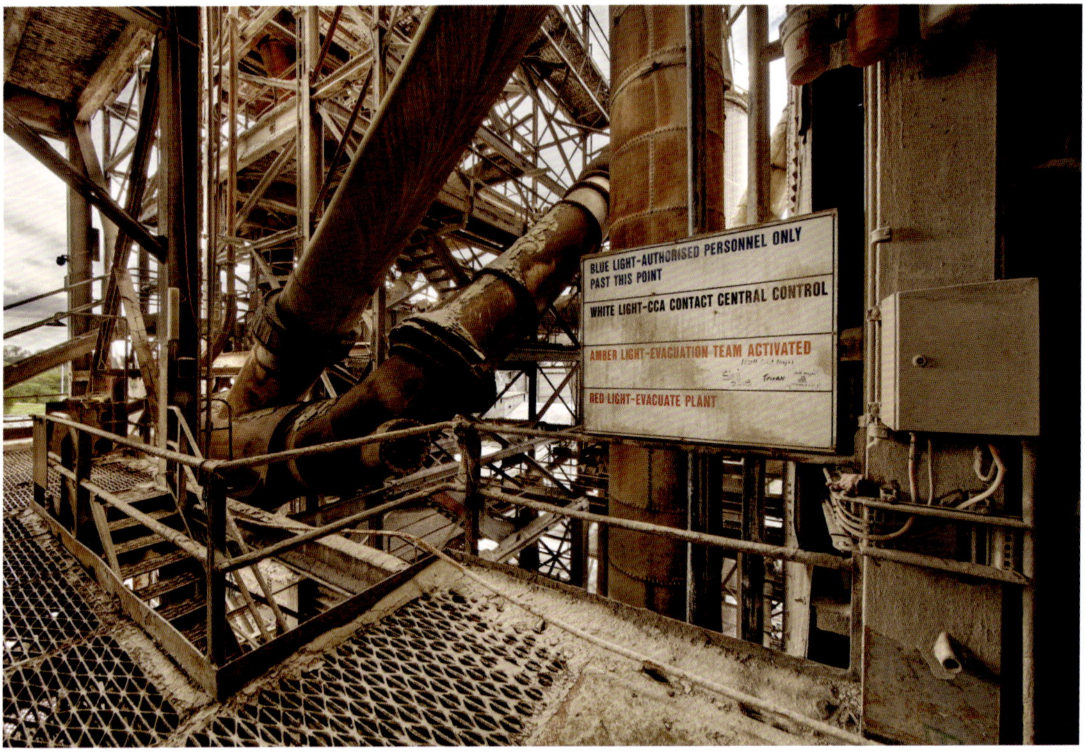

One of the factory's many upper level operating areas

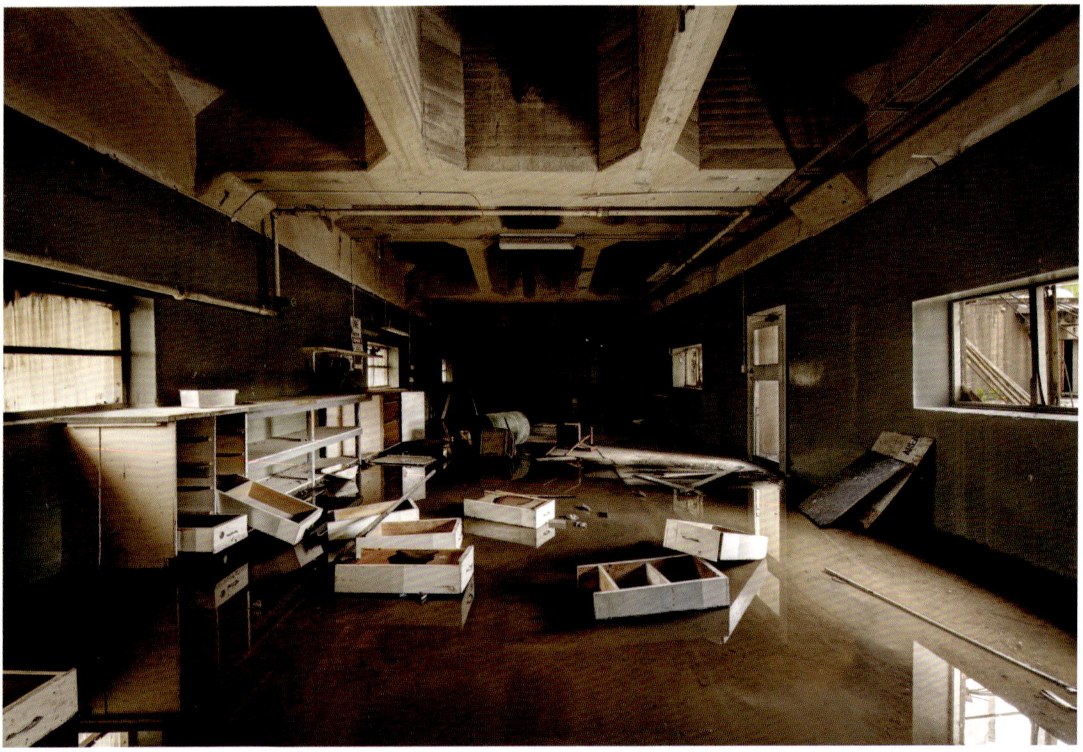

Water covers the floors of a storage space

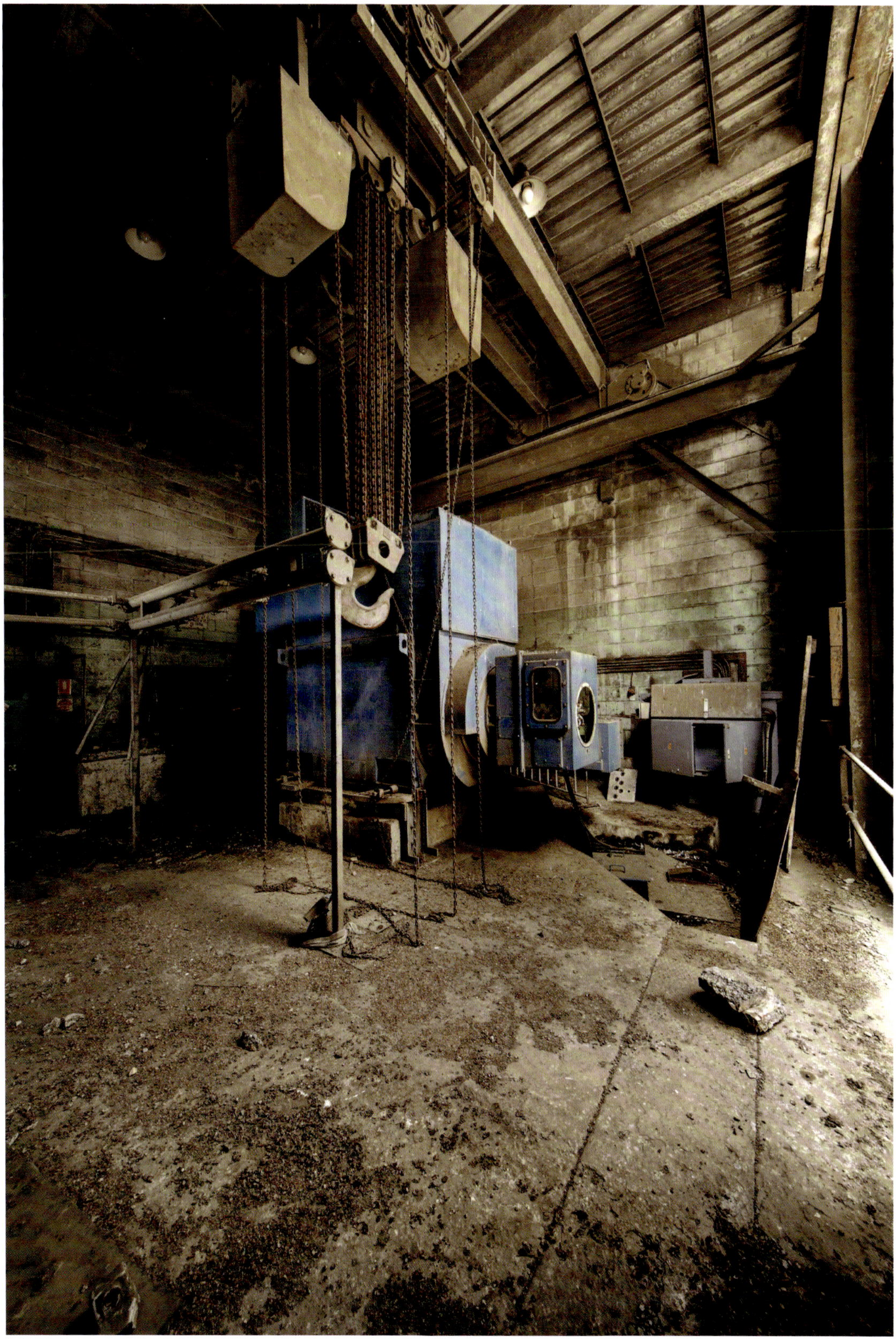

Machinery of all shapes and sizes can be found throughout the vast complex

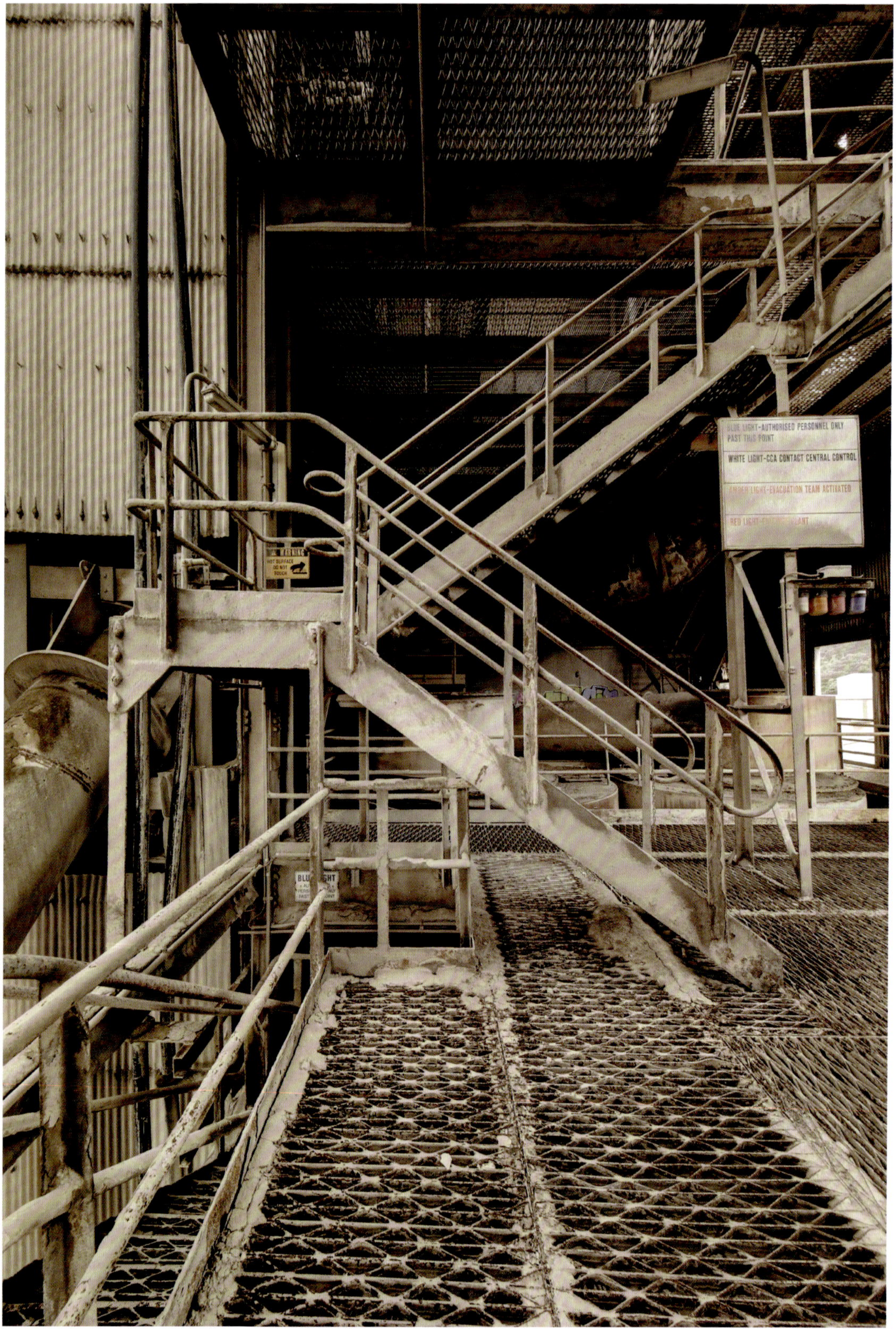

A number of stairways and ladders weave through the complex

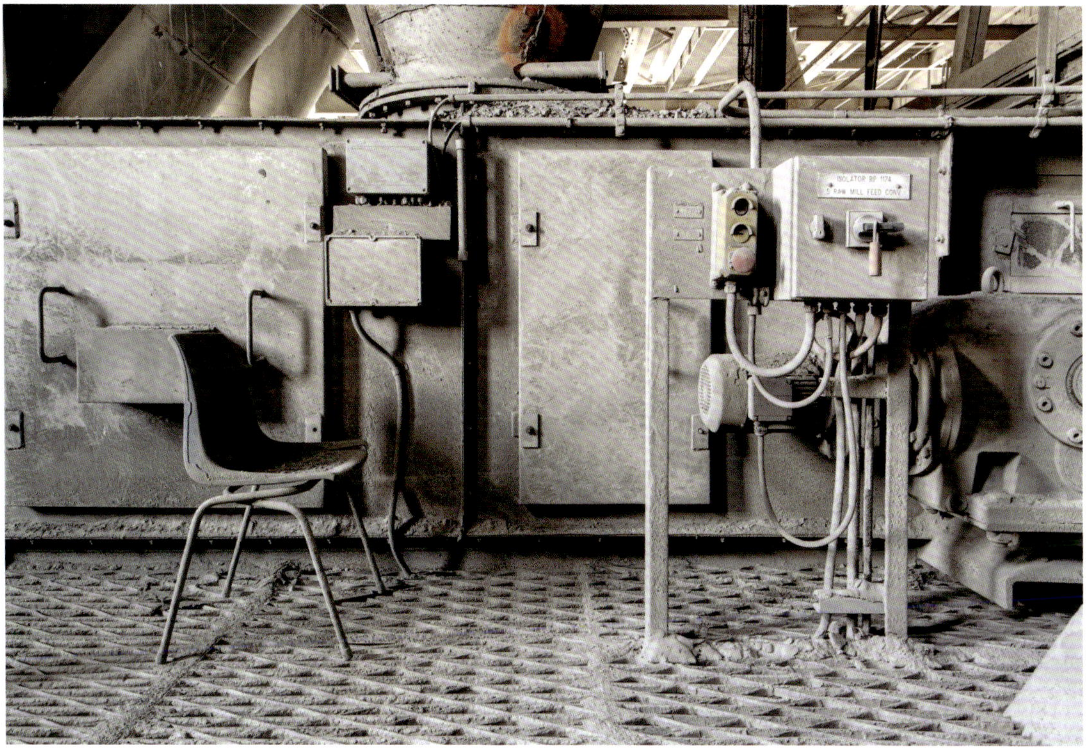

One of the factory's numerous control areas

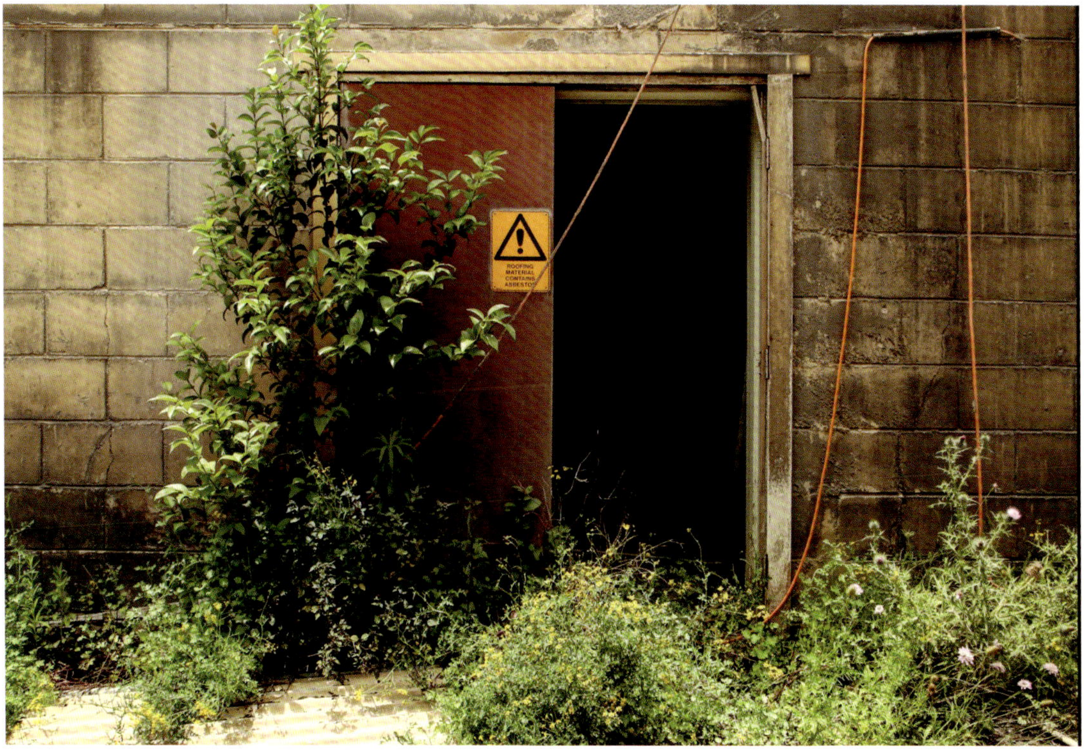

Overgrowth and plant life surrounding a dark engine room

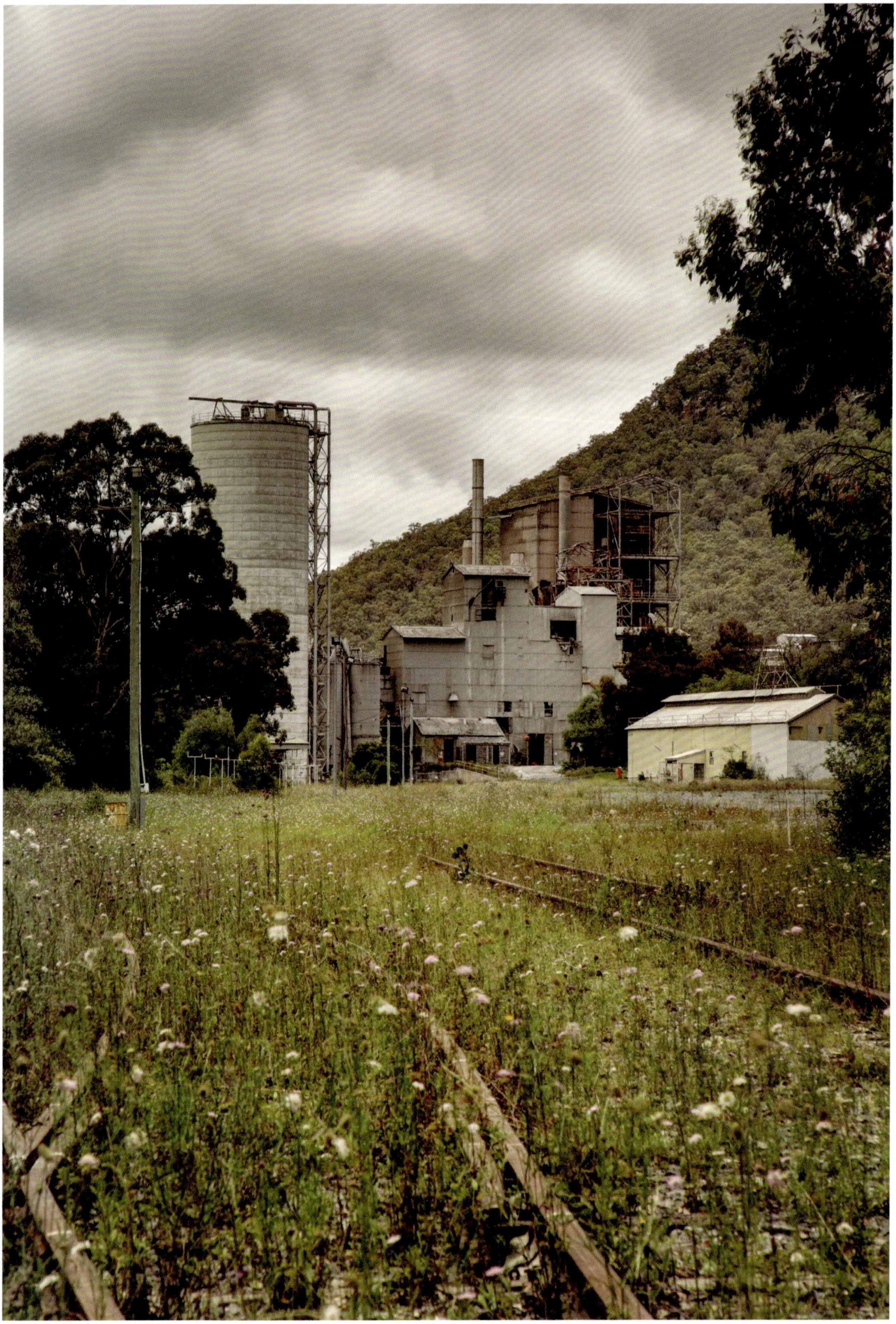

Overgrown tracks lead to the centre of the large facility

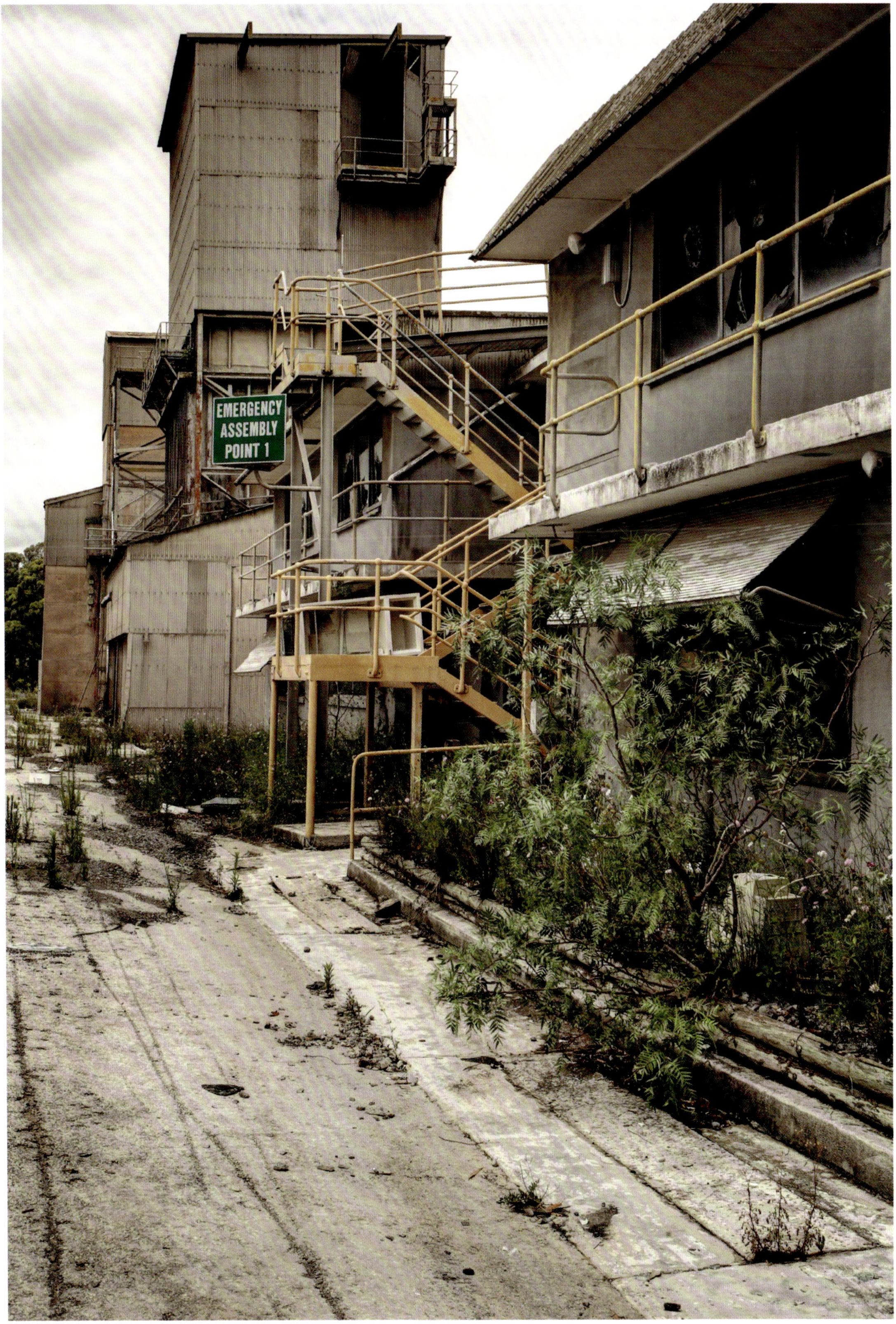

The factory's former emergency assembly area

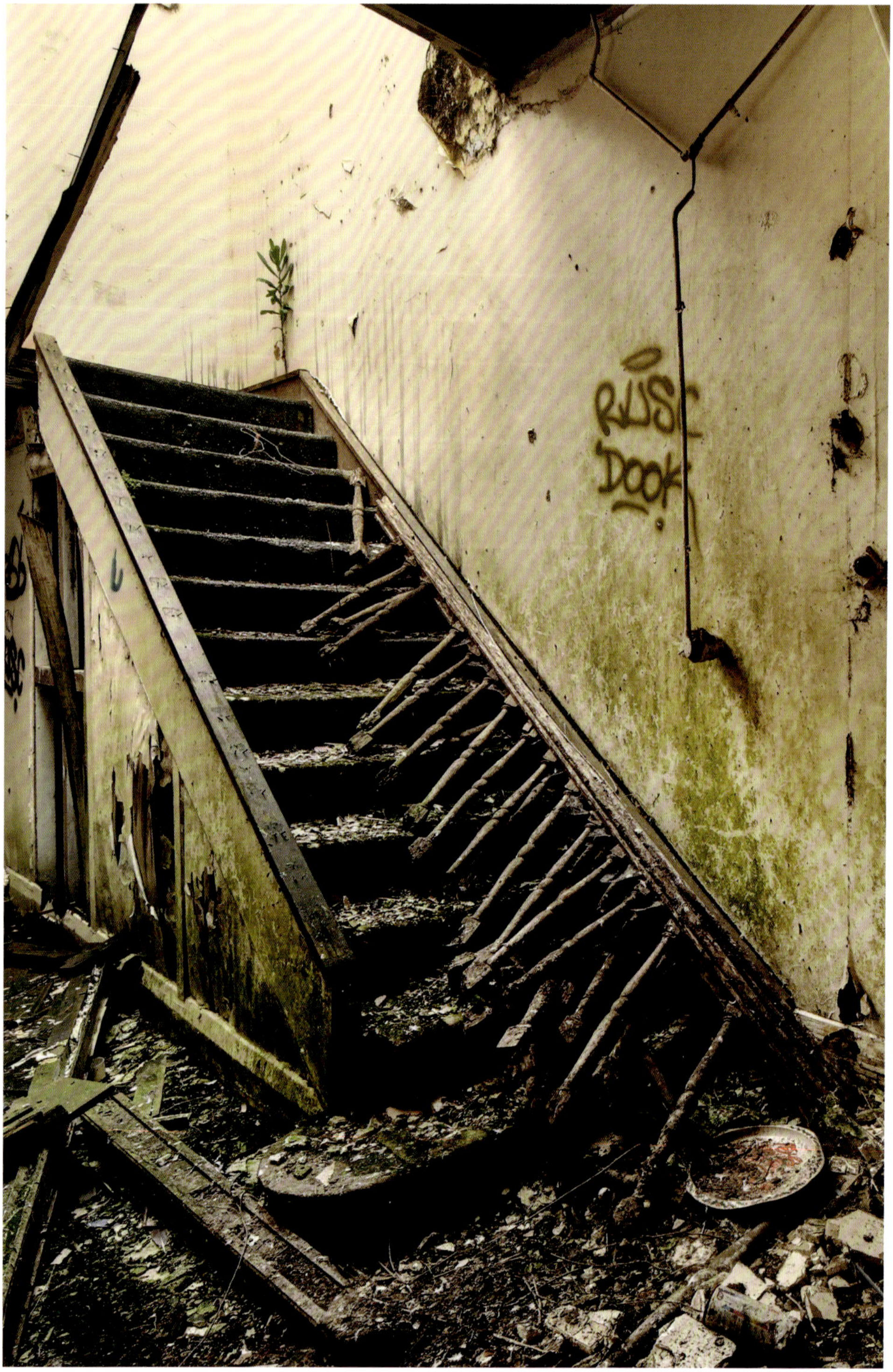

A crumbling staircase leads to the building's roofless upper level

ST JOSEPH'S CONVENT

St Joseph's Convent housed both nuns and girls, with a focus on religious instruction mixed with elements of a cross-educational curriculum. Located in the picturesque Mittagong township, the facility's long history is often threatened by rumours of demolition. Still sitting oddly and hauntingly derelict between houses filled with the warmth of families, the local community often rallies together to fend off hungry property developers.

The remains of the convent still crumble to this day, although recently an initiative was greenlighted for a proposed development for the building to be transformed into affordable housing, thus injecting life back into the dilapidated structure.

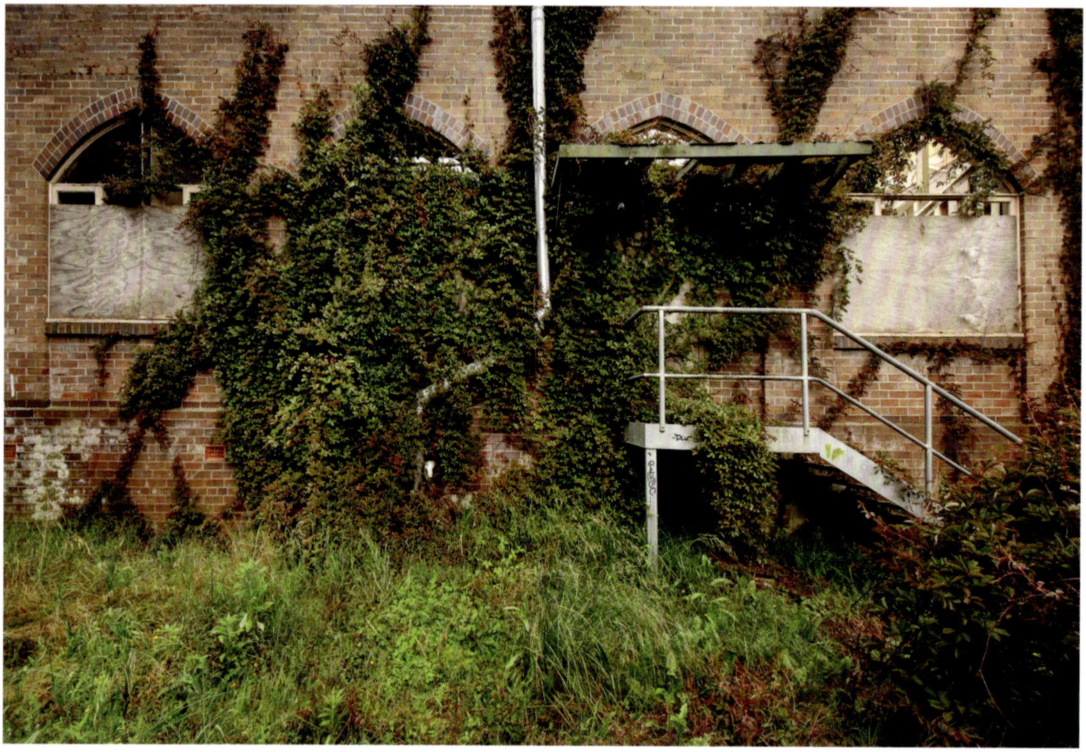

The convent's overgrown backyard

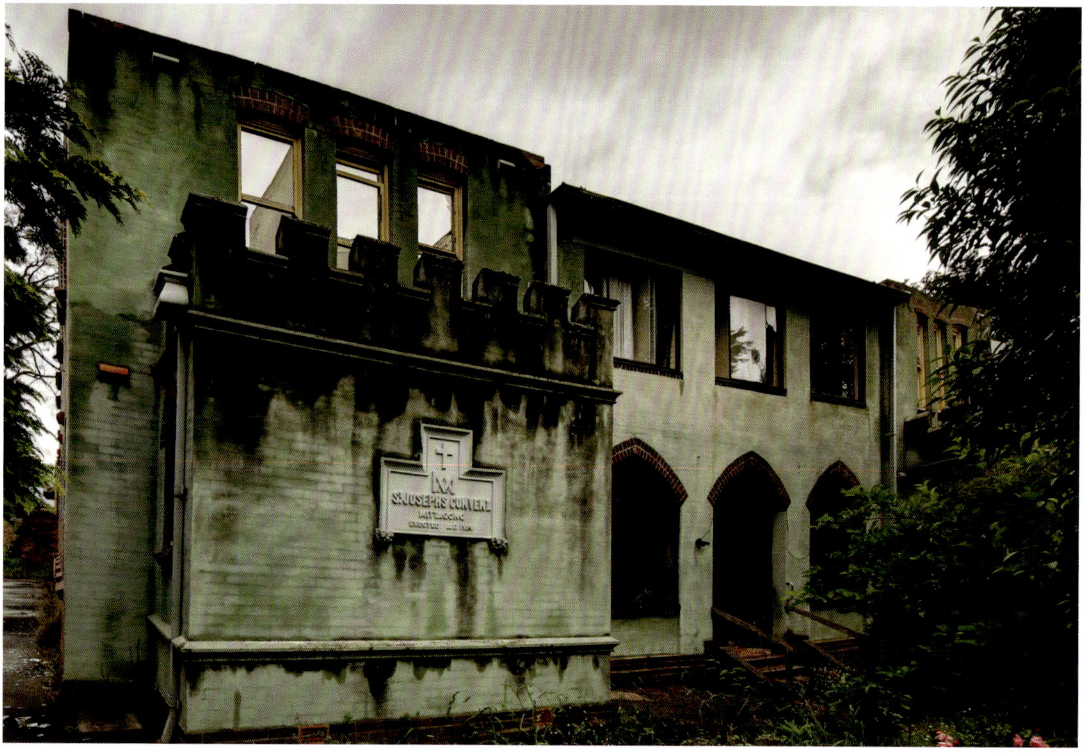

The street-facing front of the convent

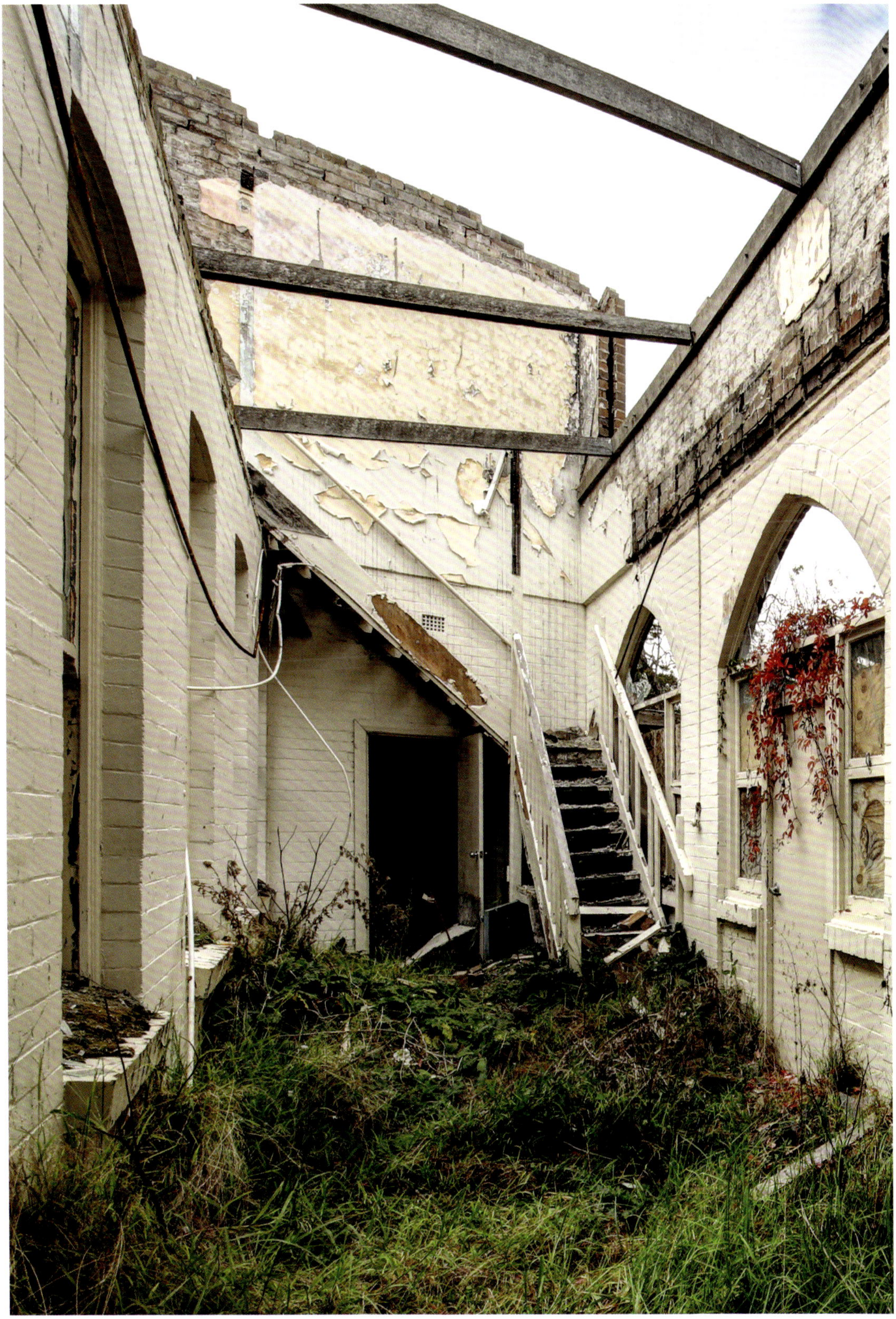

An overgrown stairway at the rear of the convent

QUEEN VICTORIA HOSPITAL

Tucked away in the quaint Blue Mountains township of Wentworth Falls, this series of dilapidated buildings form a medical facility famously known for housing a succession of tuberculosis patients. Built initially as a retreat for a wealthy businessman, the 1950s would see the structure transformed into a nursing home for the chronically ill. In 1999 the clinic closed permanently and after years of no maintenance, trees and foliage now enshroud the once-visible hospital.

Comprised of former patient wards, therapy suites, hydro baths and waiting areas, the remains of the establishment now sit in dust-covered stasis. Sold in 2012 with the aim of re-developing the space, the facility remains in a state of ruin in its picturesque location.

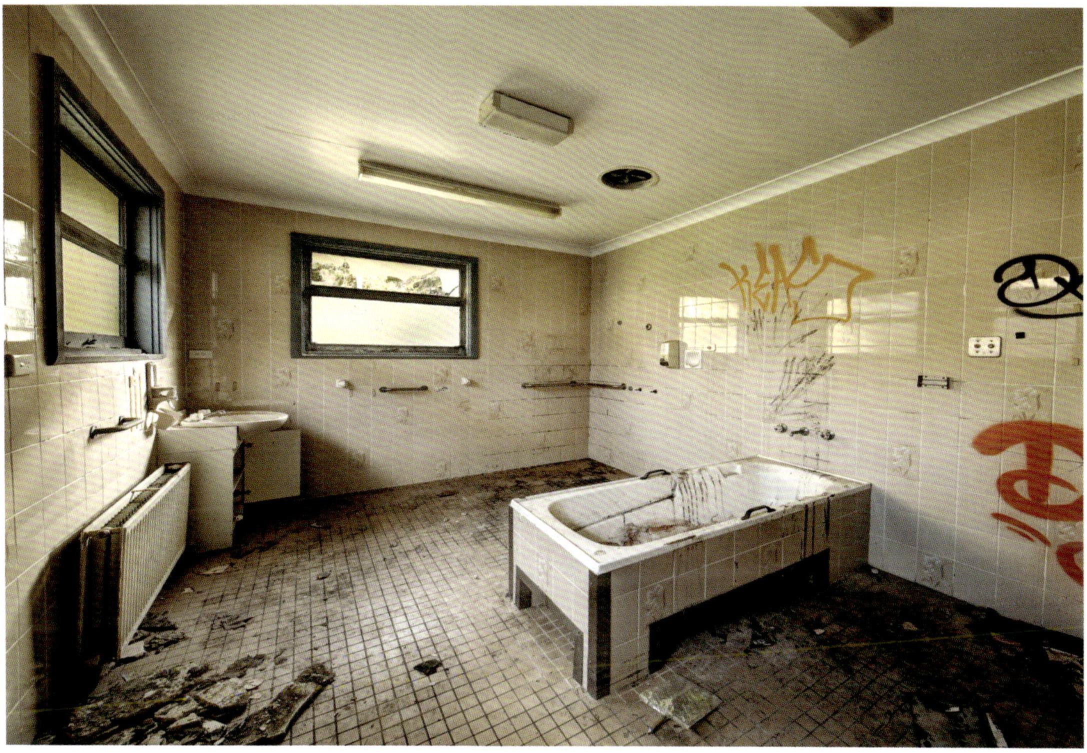

A bathtub sits in one of the facility's patient areas

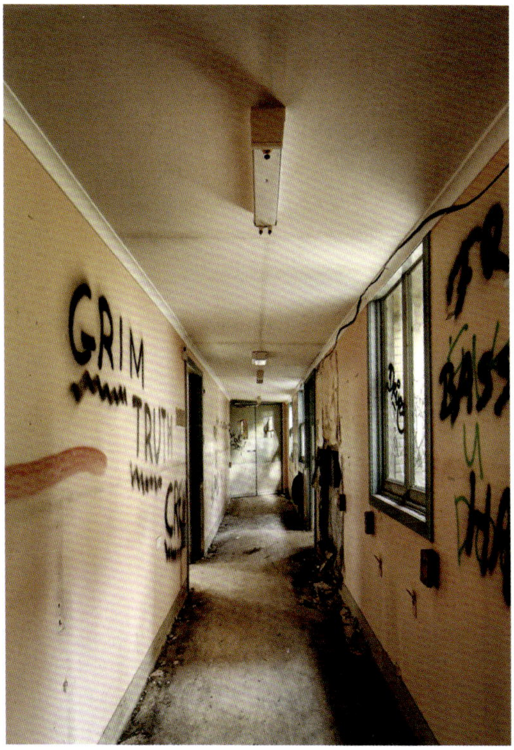

A long hallway leads to a clinical area

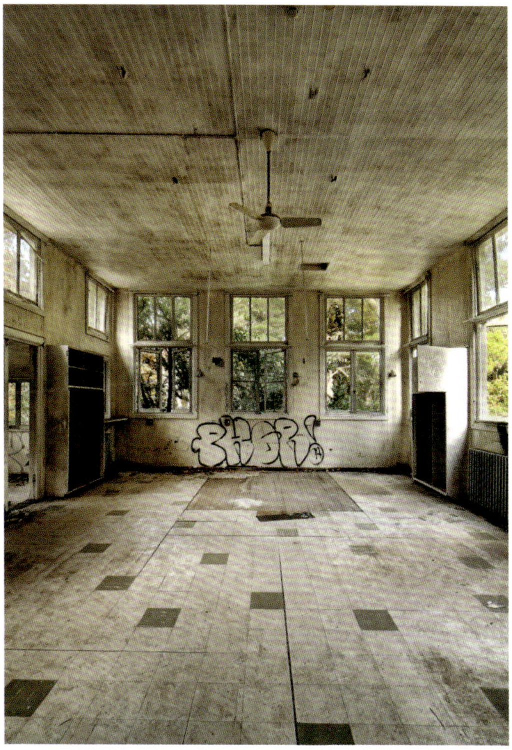

One of the former patient wards

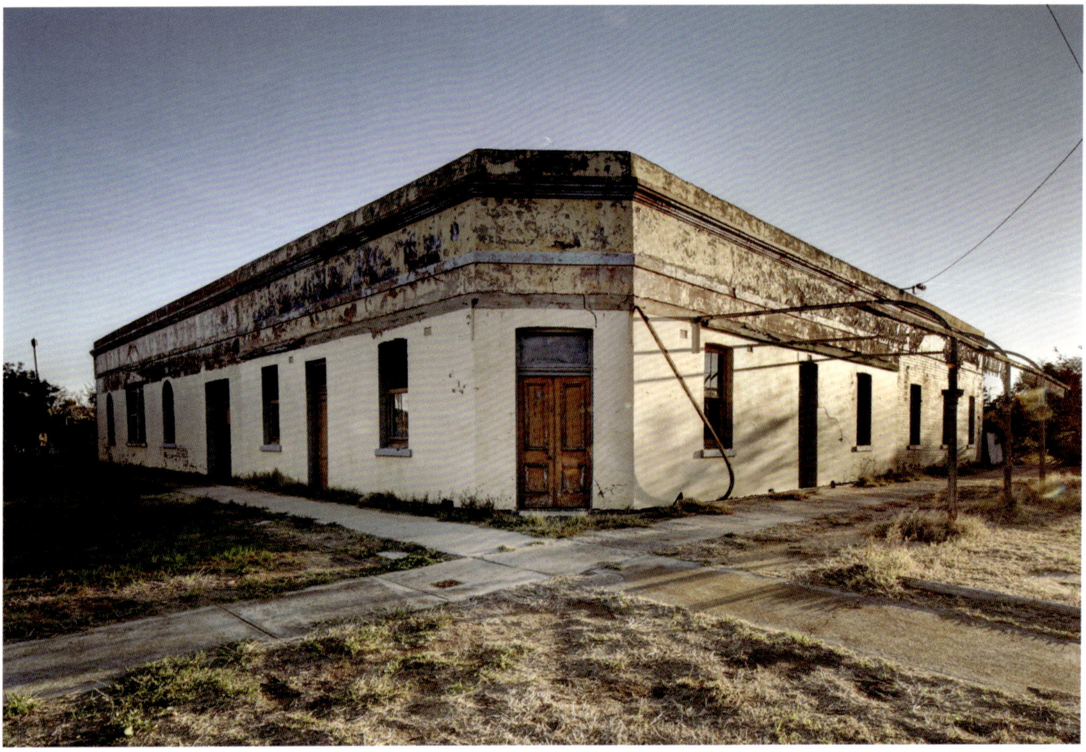

The pub's front façade; the veranda has since been removed

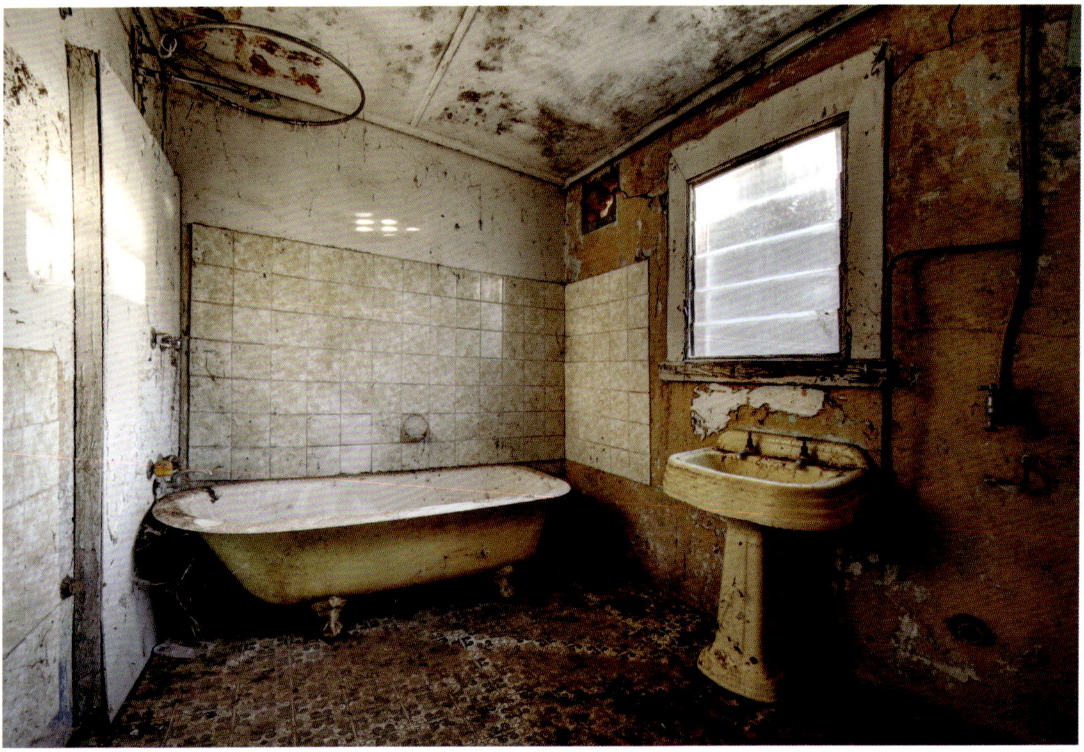

A bathtub and Art Deco wash basin towards the back of the pub

THE ROADHOUSE

Sitting idle on a street side in the central southern township of Hay, the Terminus Hotel pulled its last beer many decades ago. Established in 1880 and licensed from 1882 to 1940, the pub has undergone a succession of facelifts including as a tourist stop, retail outlet and personal residence.

Filled with all the trademarks of the great Australian vintage pub — complete with real bullet holes — the resident ghost is there to guide you through its darkened hallways, drinking spaces, guest rooms and cellars.

Purchased in 1990 with the aim of restoration, the structure proved difficult to maintain. Still in desperate need of an energetic buyer, this chunk of 'Aussie Pub' history remains in a state of disrepair.

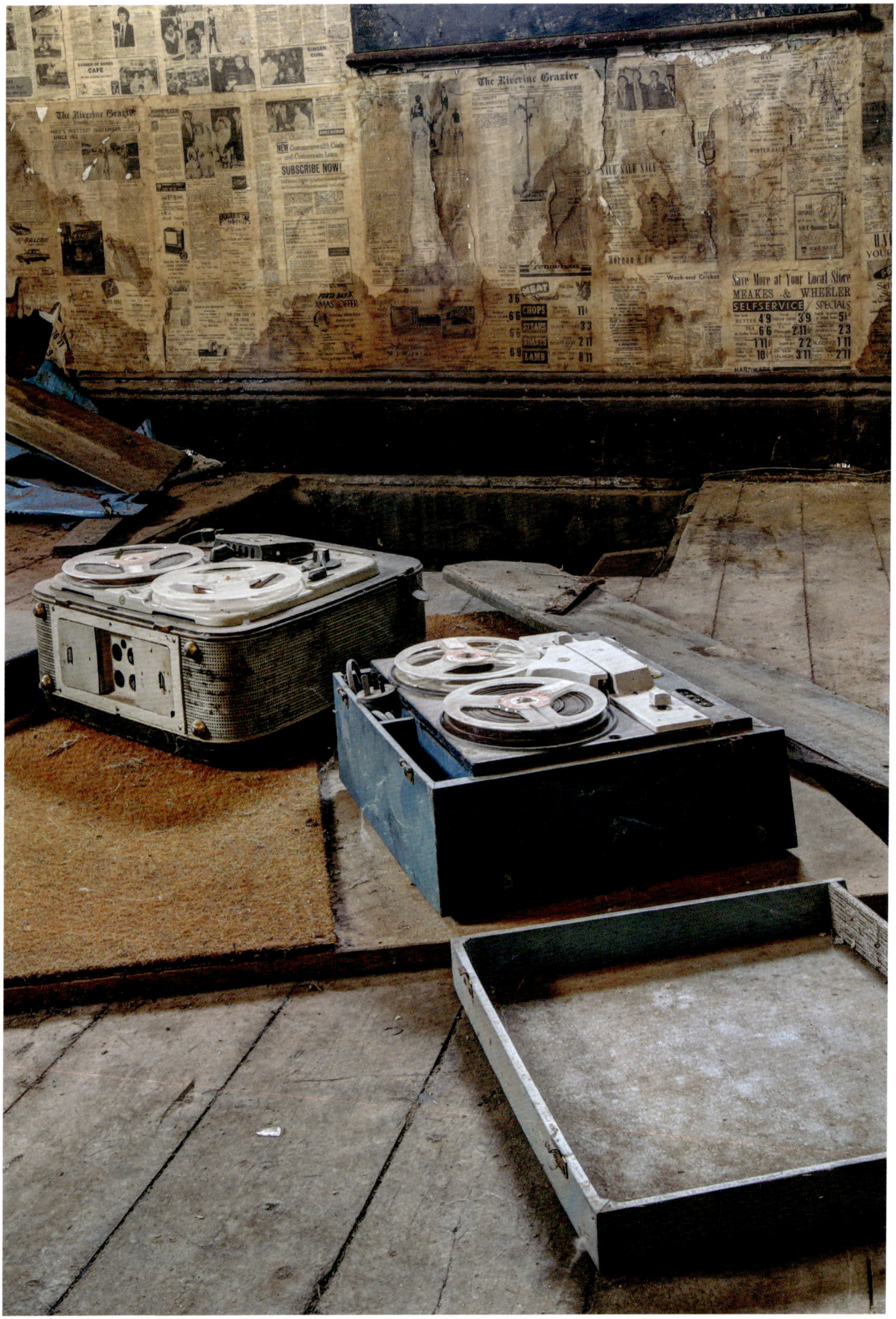

A reel-to-reel player and recorder, found on the floor of the front bar

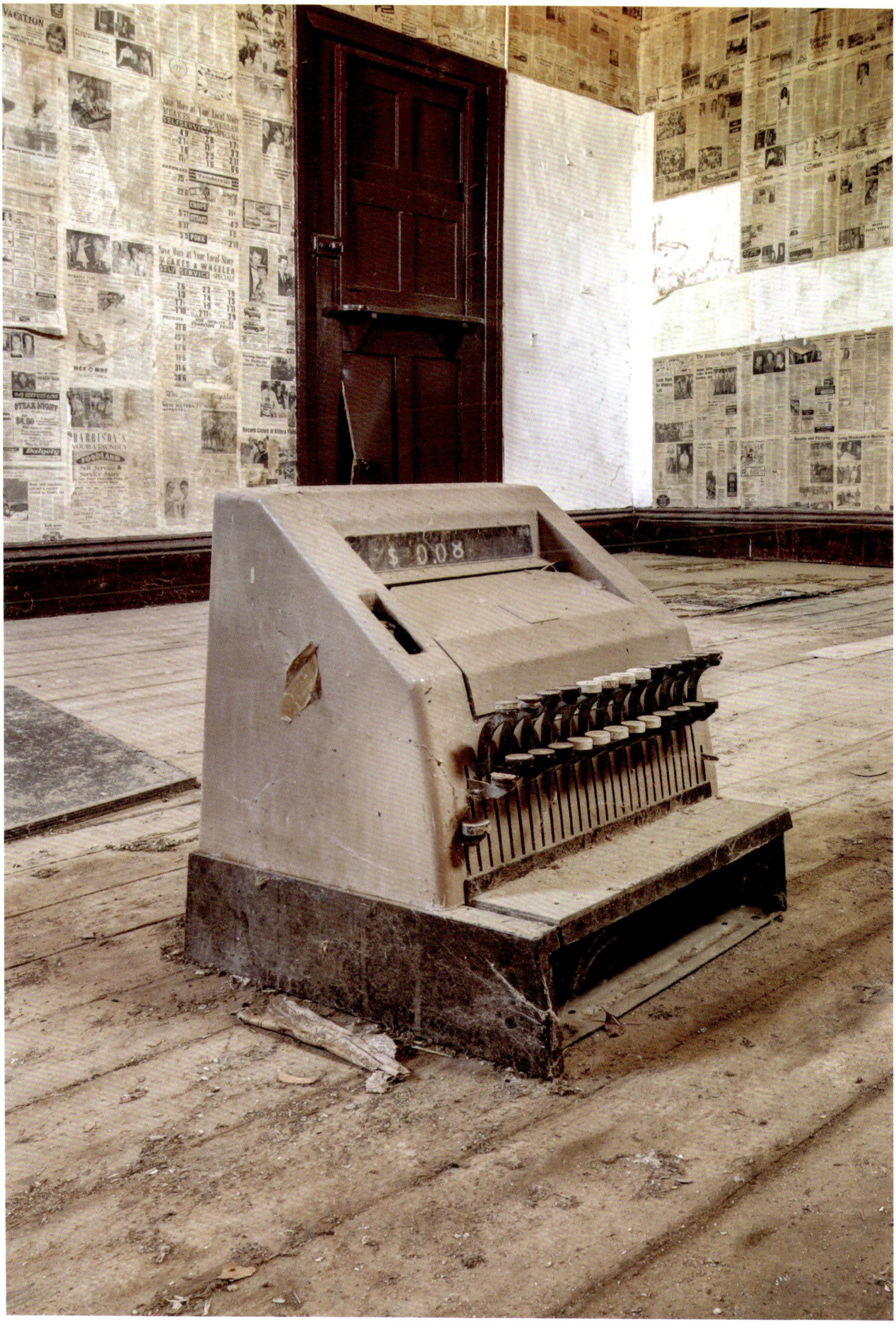

The pub's front bar contains a handful of vintage items

BALMAIN LEAGUES CLUB

Sitting in a state of prolonged inactivity, this infamous sporting facility closed its doors permanently in 2010. Built in 1957, the club entered into voluntary administration as a result of severe financial difficulty. This ugly urban eye-sore was then rendered unusable after a series of fires and countless acts of vandalism.

Debris litters the damp floors of former convention and reception spaces surrounded by charred and blackened walls. A 90s-era vintage internet kiosk sits in the shadows, filled with smashed monitors and keyboards. Outside, the club's winding concrete car park is an unintentional street art gallery with works left by some of Sydney's most talented graffiti experts.

A much sought-after inner Sydney real estate space, this now crumbing concrete ruin is yet to make way for a proposed mix-use development project.

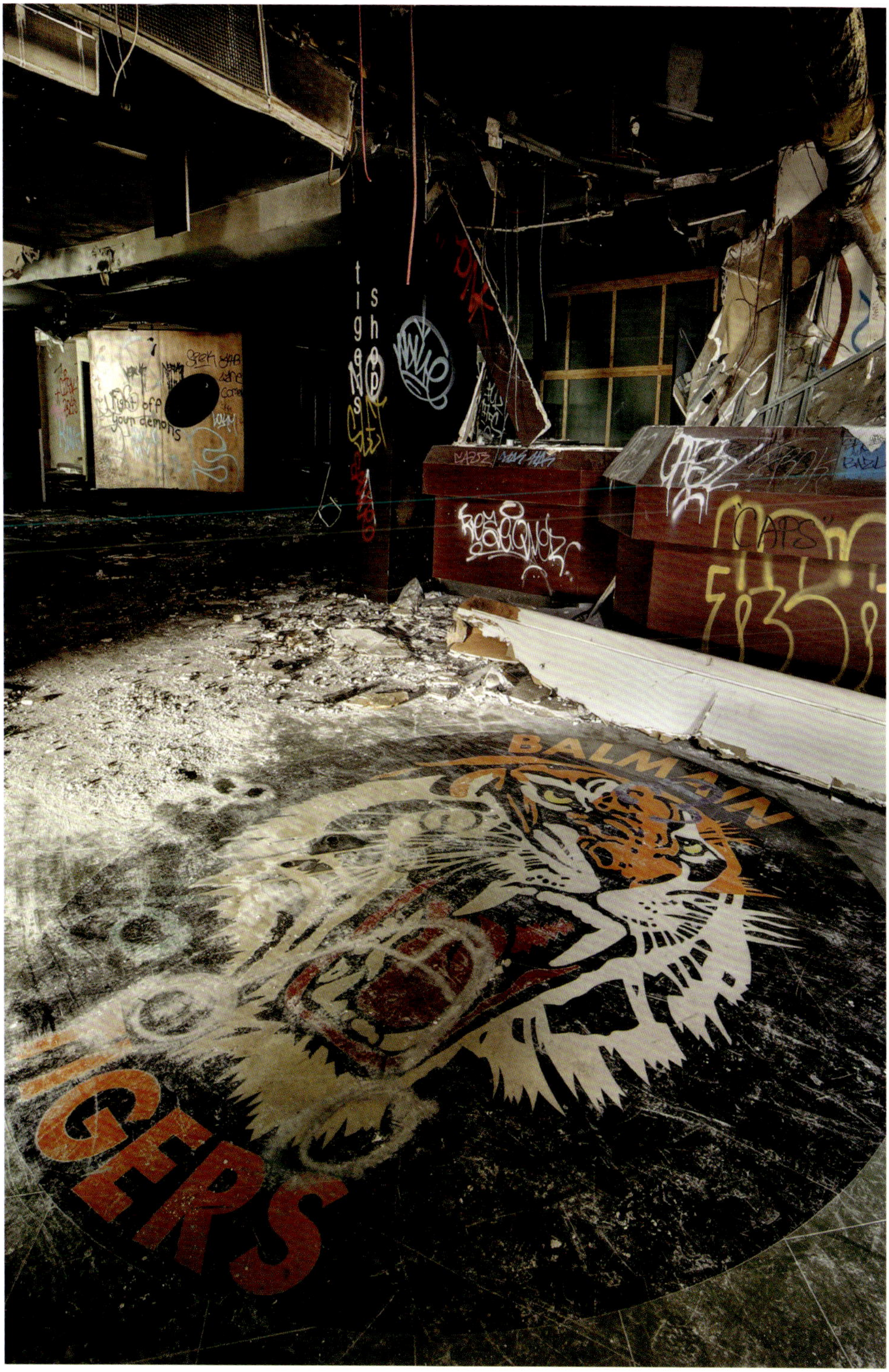

The dust-covered Balmain Tigers logo on the floor of the sporting club

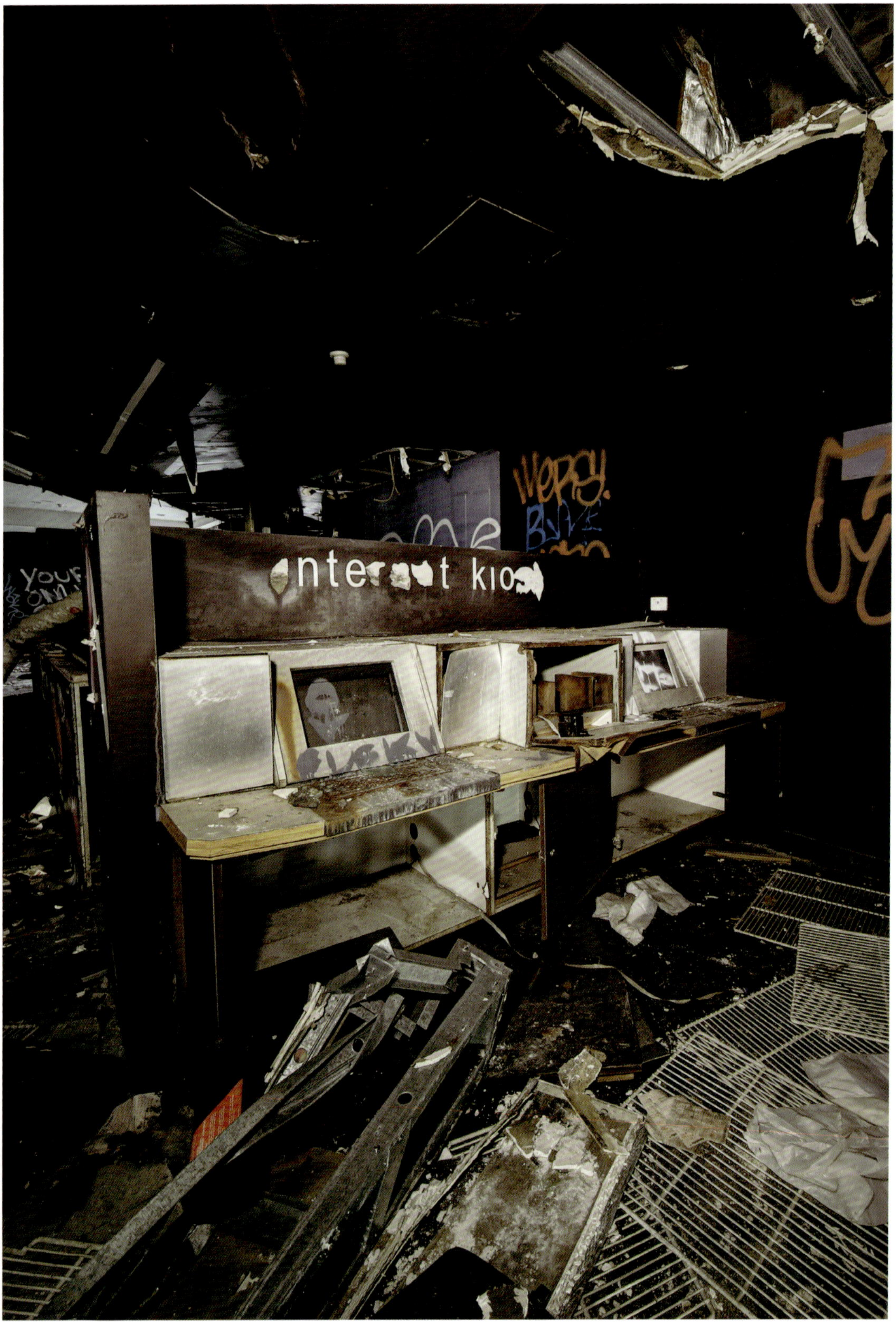

Prior to the smartphone era, internet kiosks were a common feature in many establishments

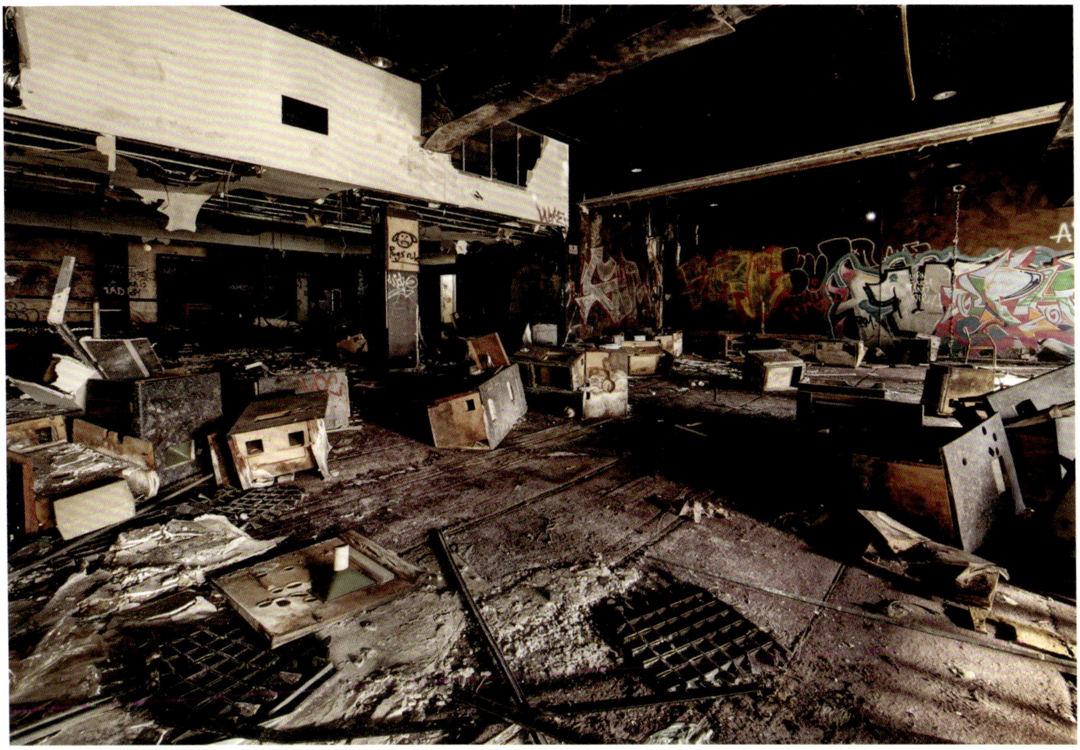

A debris-covered central function space

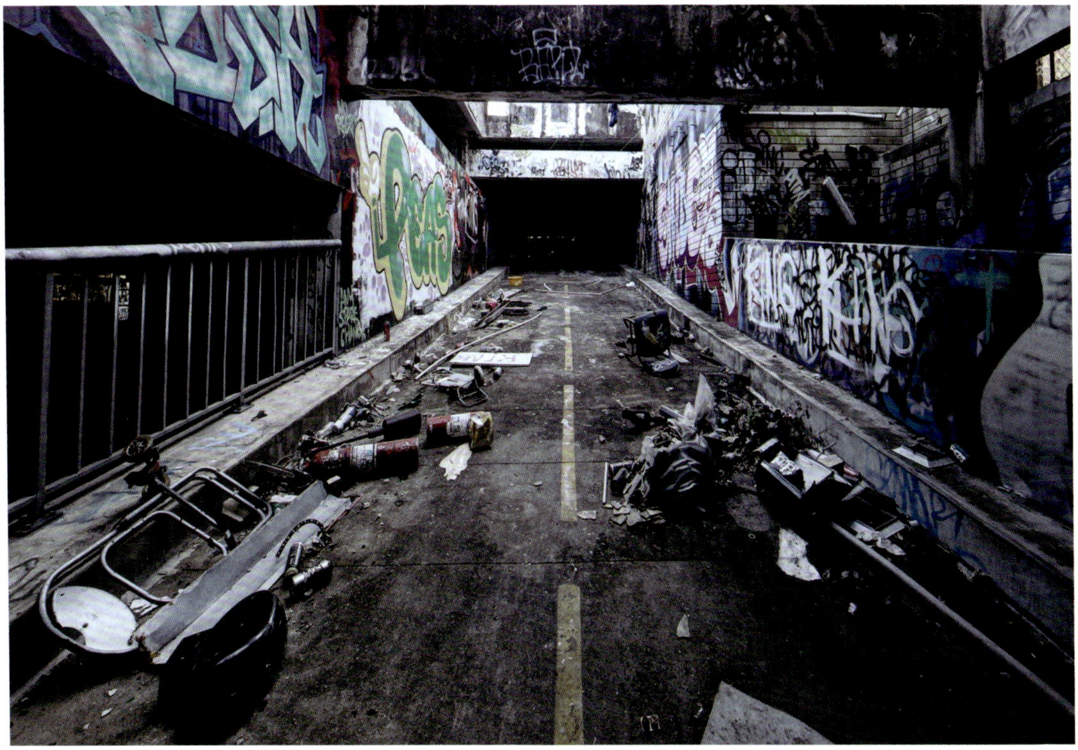

The gloomy car park has become an unintentional street art gallery

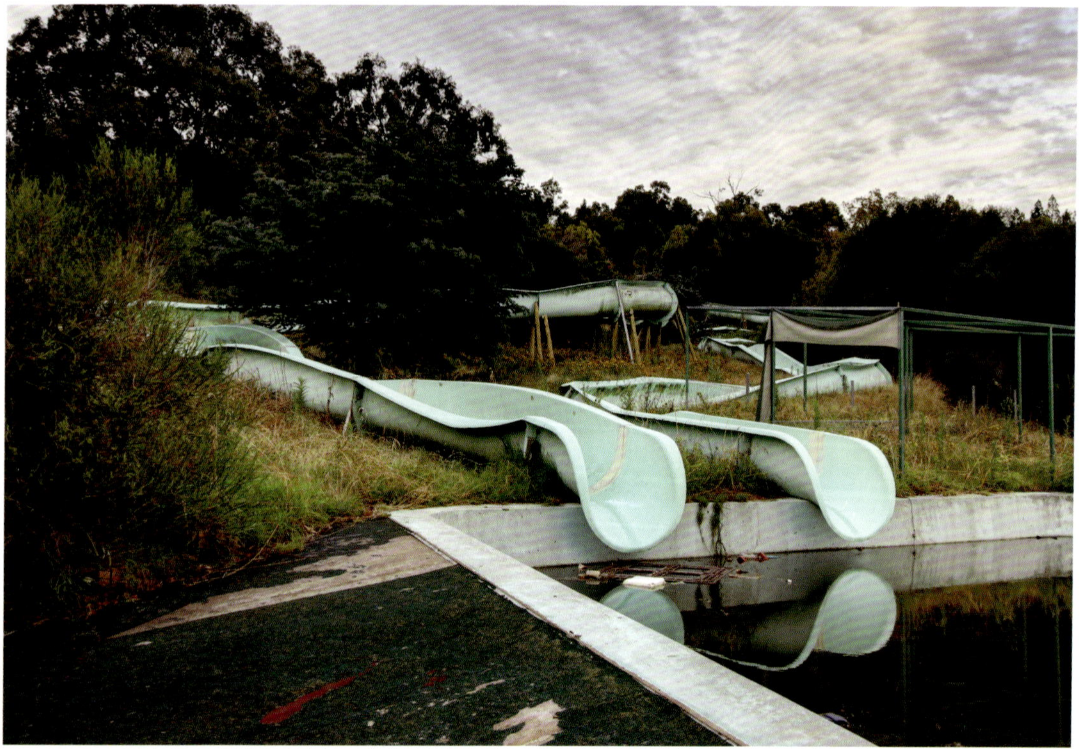

The slime-filled splash pool

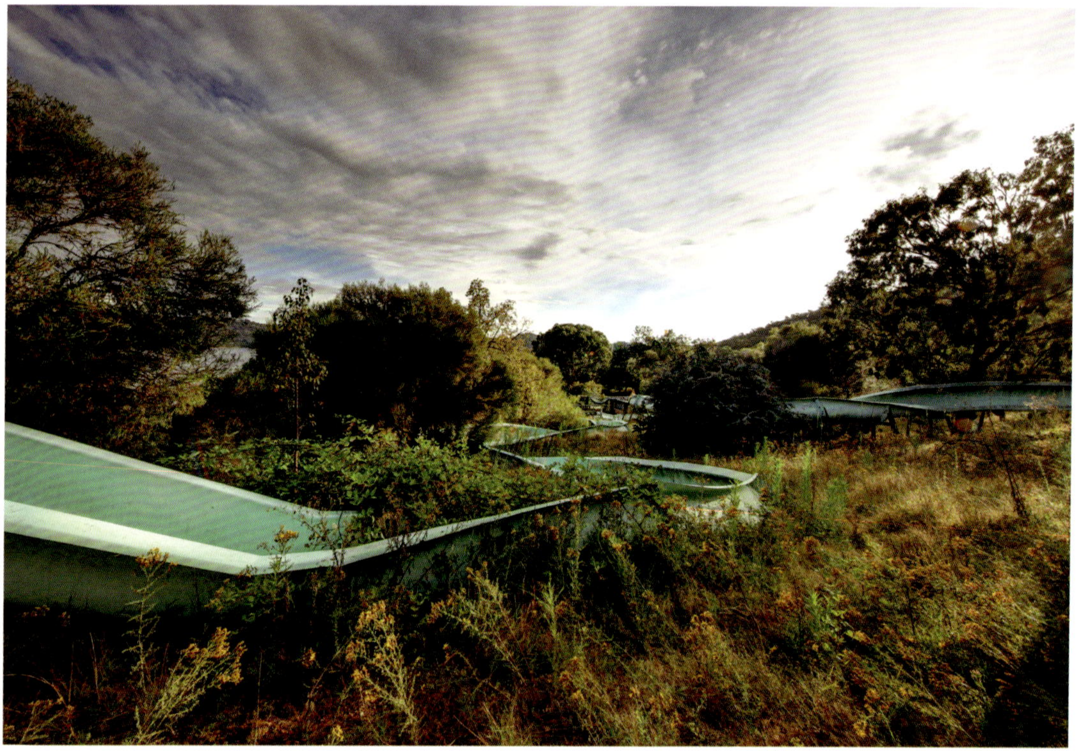

The body of the main waterslide weaves through foliage on a picturesque hillside

THE WATERSLIDE

Stretching downwards on an overgrown hillside, this long abandoned fibreglass waterslide weaves through overgrown bushes, trees and shrubs. Located beside a campground lined with cabins and other long-stay establishments, the last screaming punter made their final splash many years back. Slime and mud now cake the landing pools that once sparkled and shimmered in the New South Wales sun.

TRAINS

With 80s and 90s graffiti still etched into the walls, these abandoned carriages once lugged workers, school kids and general commuters to their daily destinations. With mould now covering waterlogged seats, the maps on the walls speak of more dynamic days when people watched the inner-city suburbs speed past.

Comprised of fibreglass walls and ceilings lined with latent fluorescent light bulbs, the carriages' seating areas accommodated patrons who usually travelled face-to-face on cushioned benches that ran down a narrow central aisle. Built to facilitate the city's growing population, many Sydney carriages were two stories high.

Sitting idle in a field, these forgotten train wrecks are shrouded in high grass. Becoming homes for the birds and possums, they are each filled with memories of bygone decades.

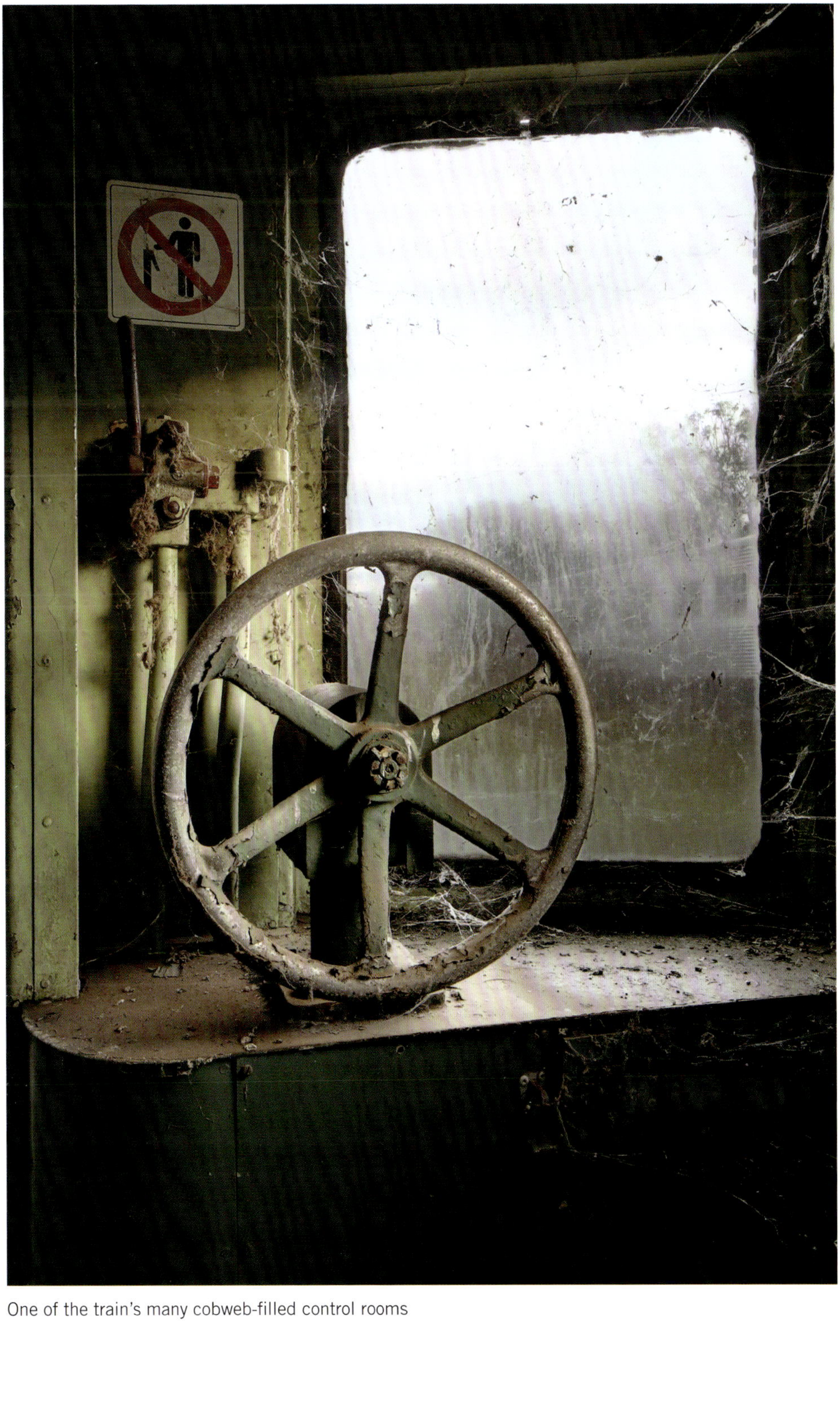

One of the train's many cobweb-filled control rooms

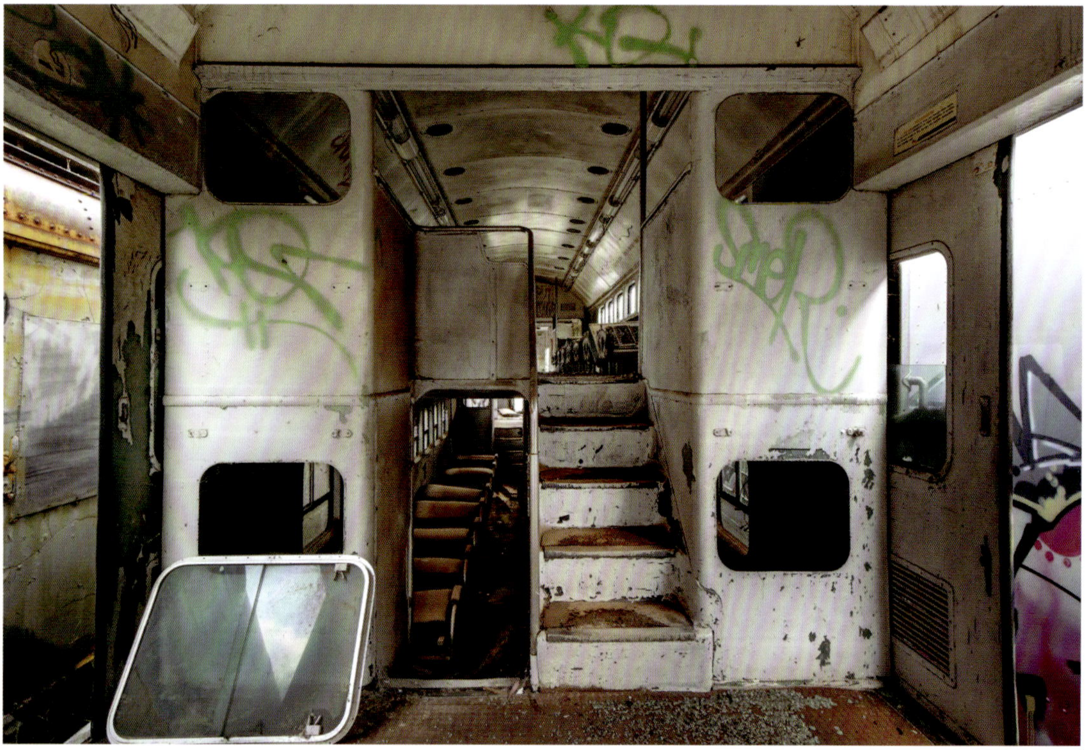

One of Sydney's many double-decker carriages

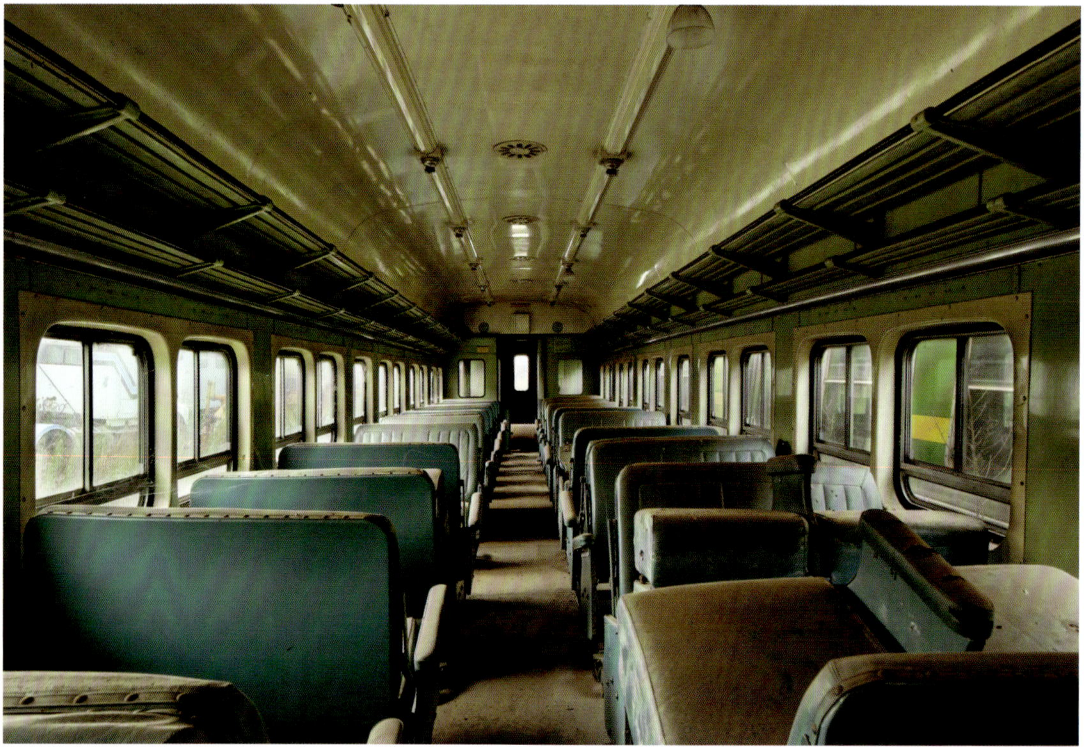

A dust-filled carriage

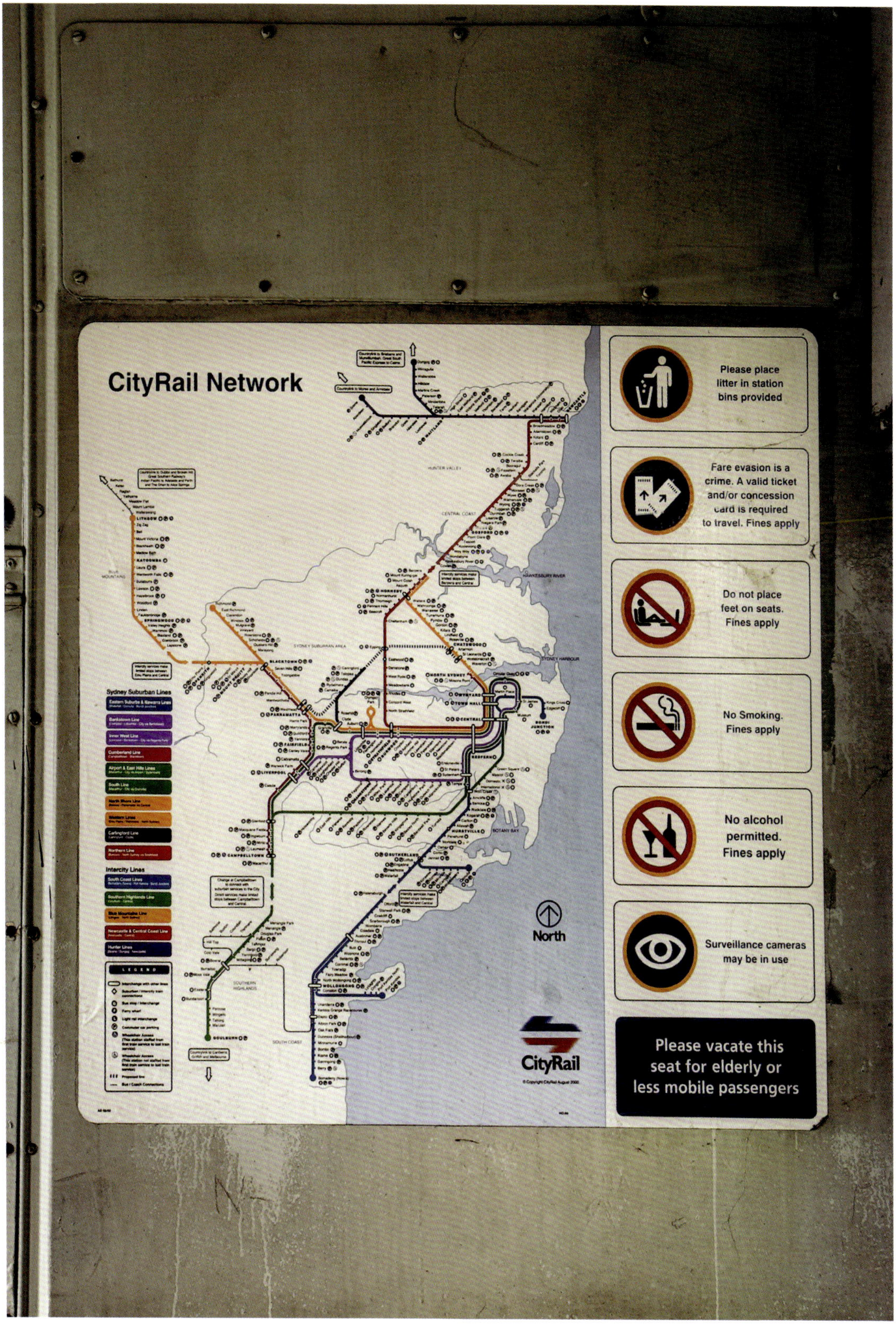

The entrance to a carriage still includes a map of Sydney's rail network

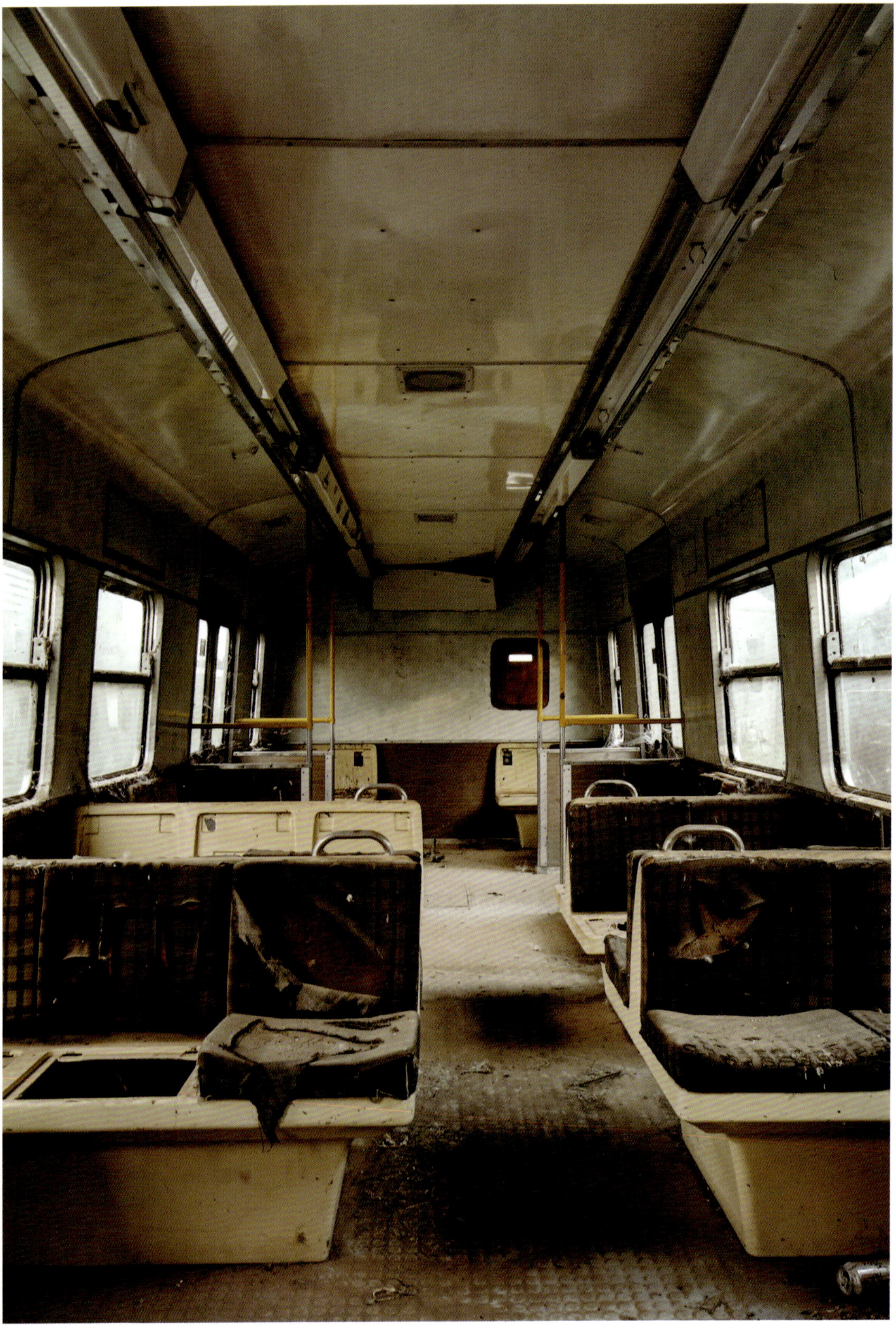

Now located in NSW, this abandoned carriage belonged to the Melbourne rail network

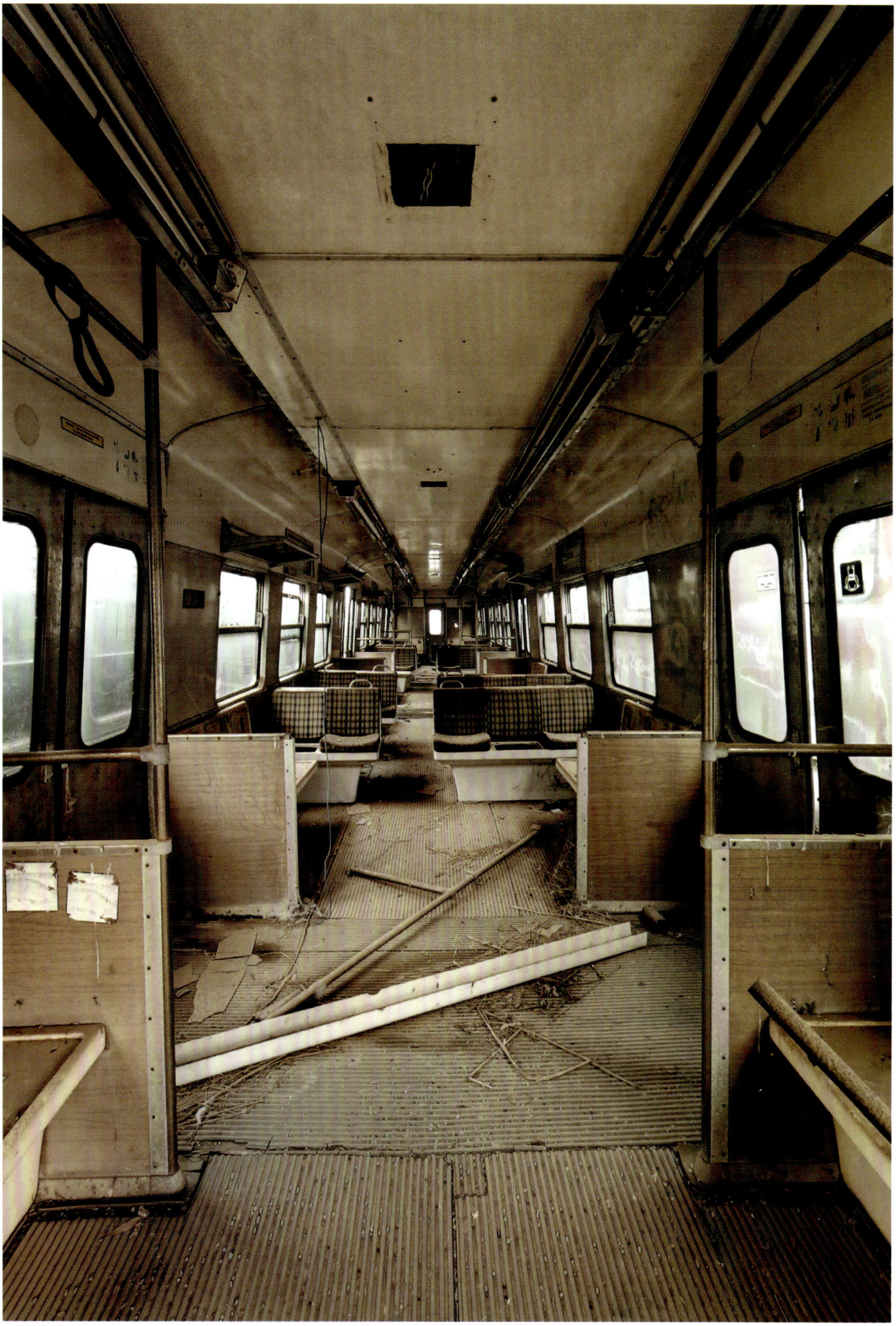

Another Melbourne carriage sitting abandoned in NSW

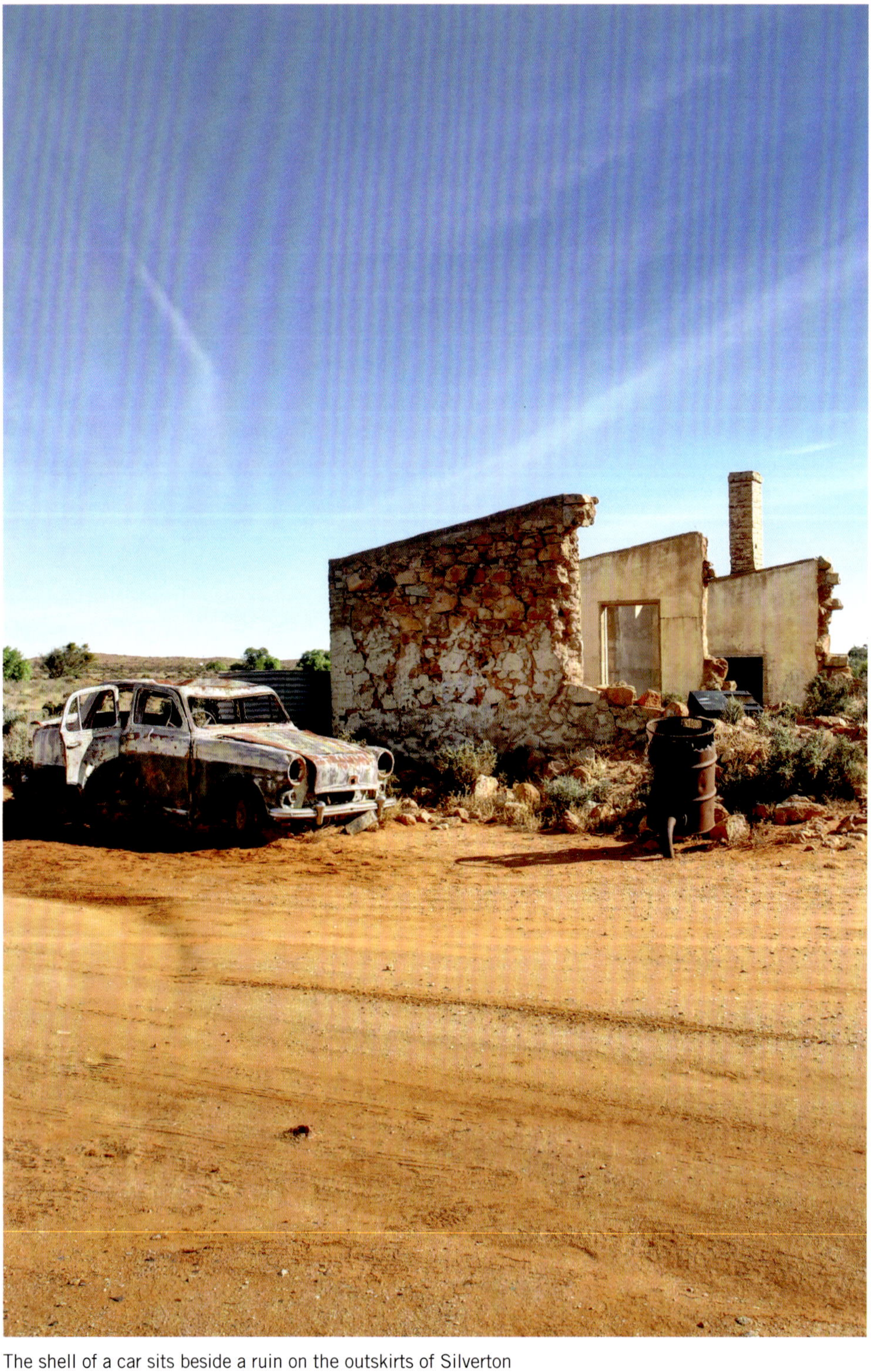

The shell of a car sits beside a ruin on the outskirts of Silverton

SILVERTON AND THE BROKEN HILL REGION

Located in the state's western desert region, the sand-filled township of Silverton includes a hotel, pub, bakery and a cluster of stone ruins scattered along its central streets. Acquiring most of its revenue from the thousands of tourists who visit this quirky spot each year, the area offers the visitor an outer desert experience, whilst at the same time remaining comfortably close to the neighbouring and much larger township of Broken Hill.

Rich silver deposits drew the first post-colonial settlers to the area but as its resources were depleted, the once-active settlement became a ghost town.

Slightly northwest of its urban grid, the Silverton cemetery is the final resting place for a handful of Australian post-colonial pioneers — the forgotten boneyard being a harsh reminder of the savage living conditions experienced by those who came to dwell here. Perhaps the town's most exciting attraction is the Mad Max 2 Museum. Filled with thousands of the famous franchise's cinematic relics, this celebration of all things post-apocalyptic is the perfect spot to commence or complete an Australian desert journey.

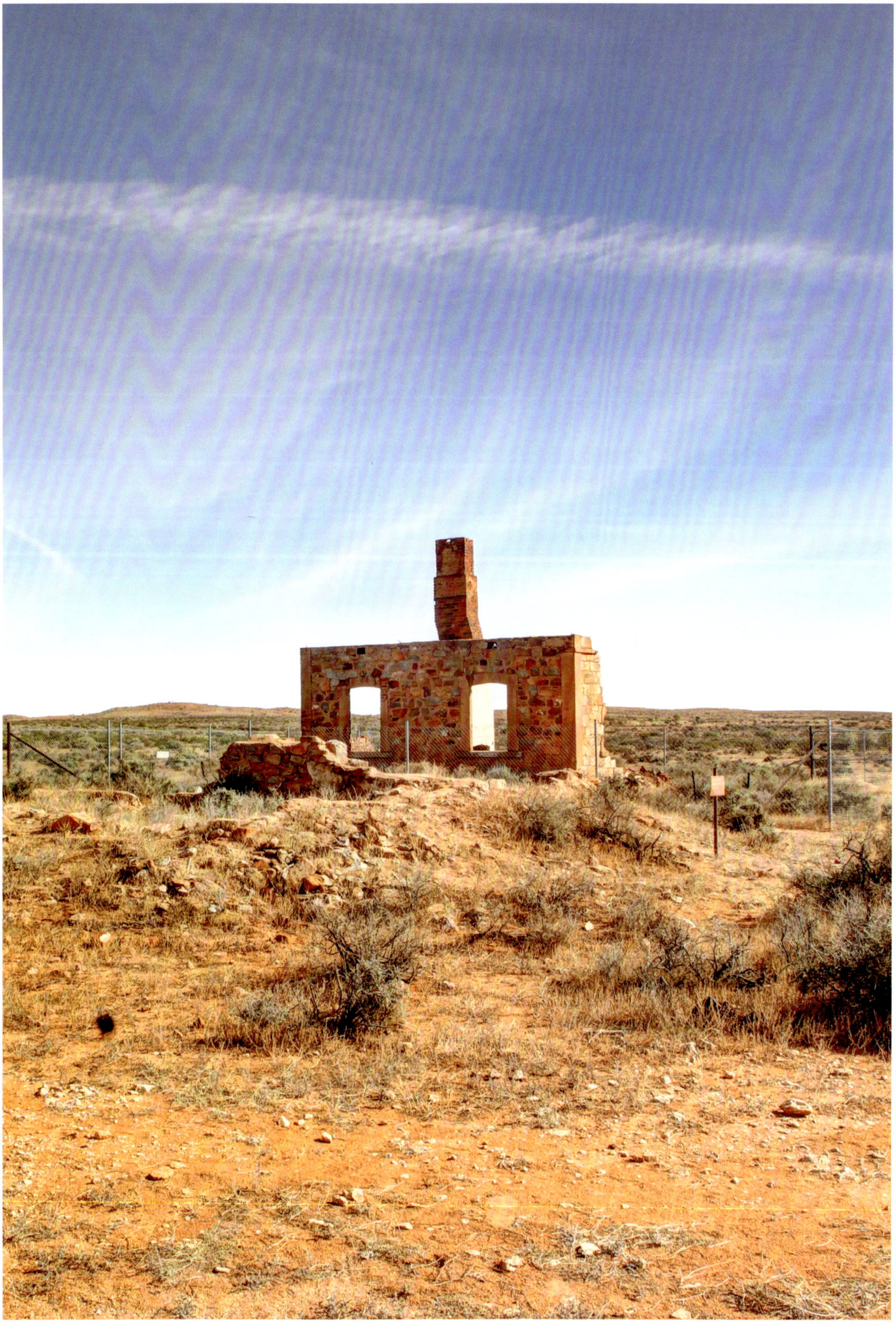

Located behind the Mad Max Museum, the chimney on this unstable ruin is about to topple

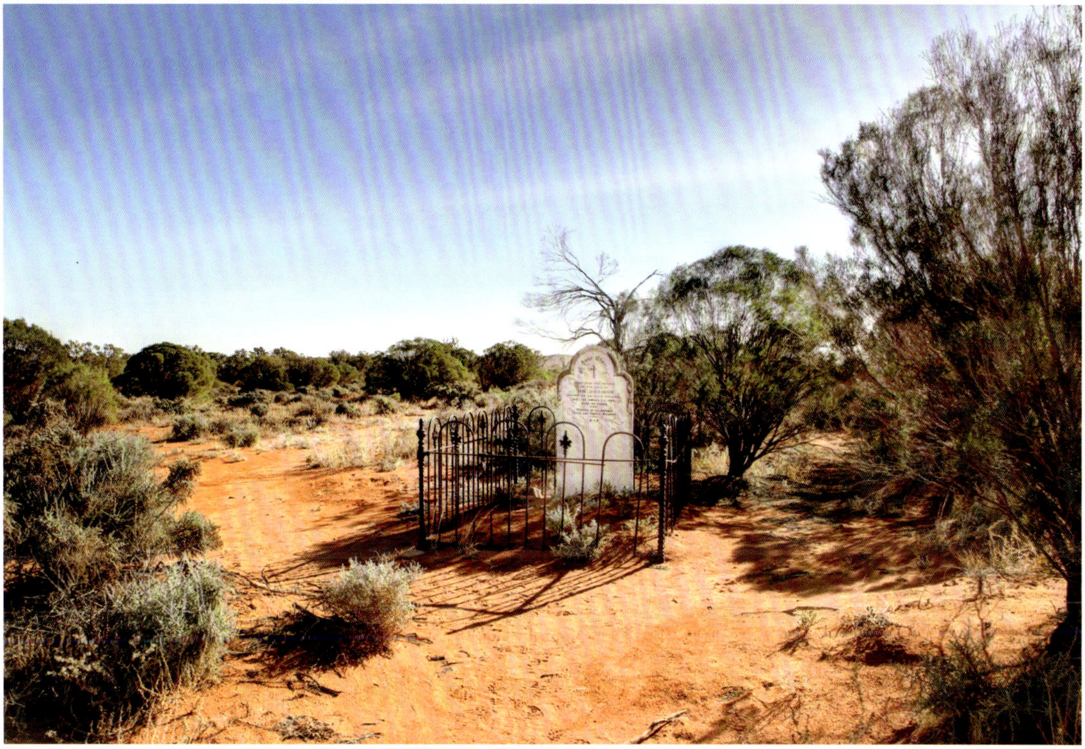

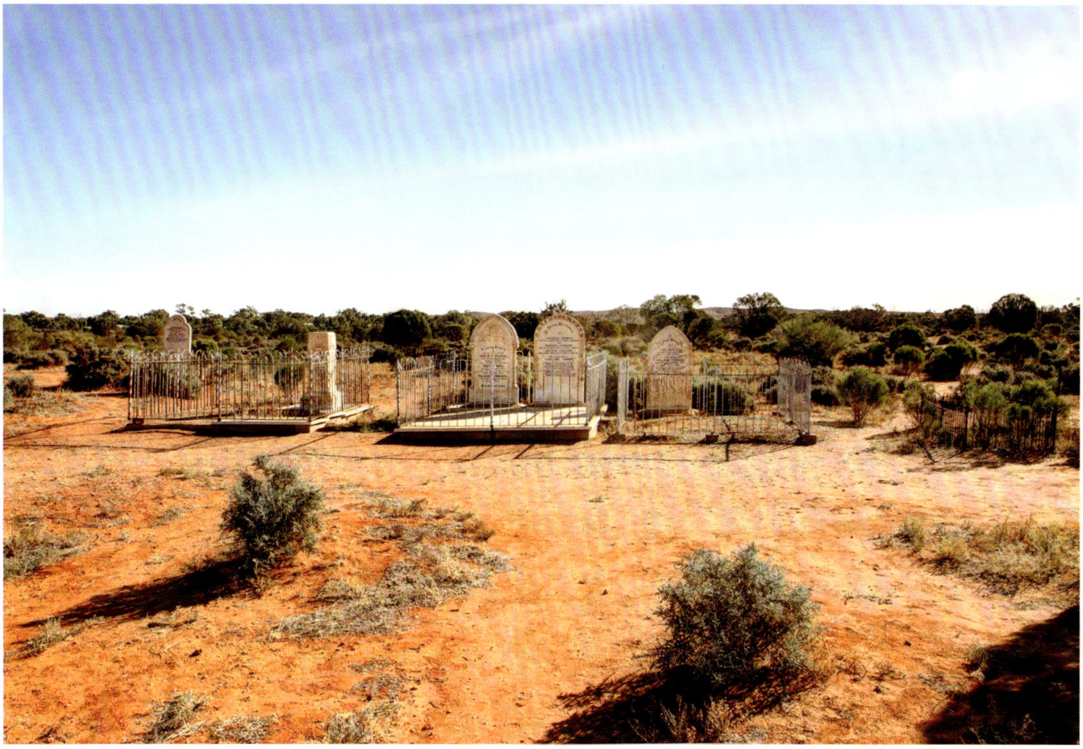

The peaceful yet sombre Silverton cemetery houses the bones of former residents

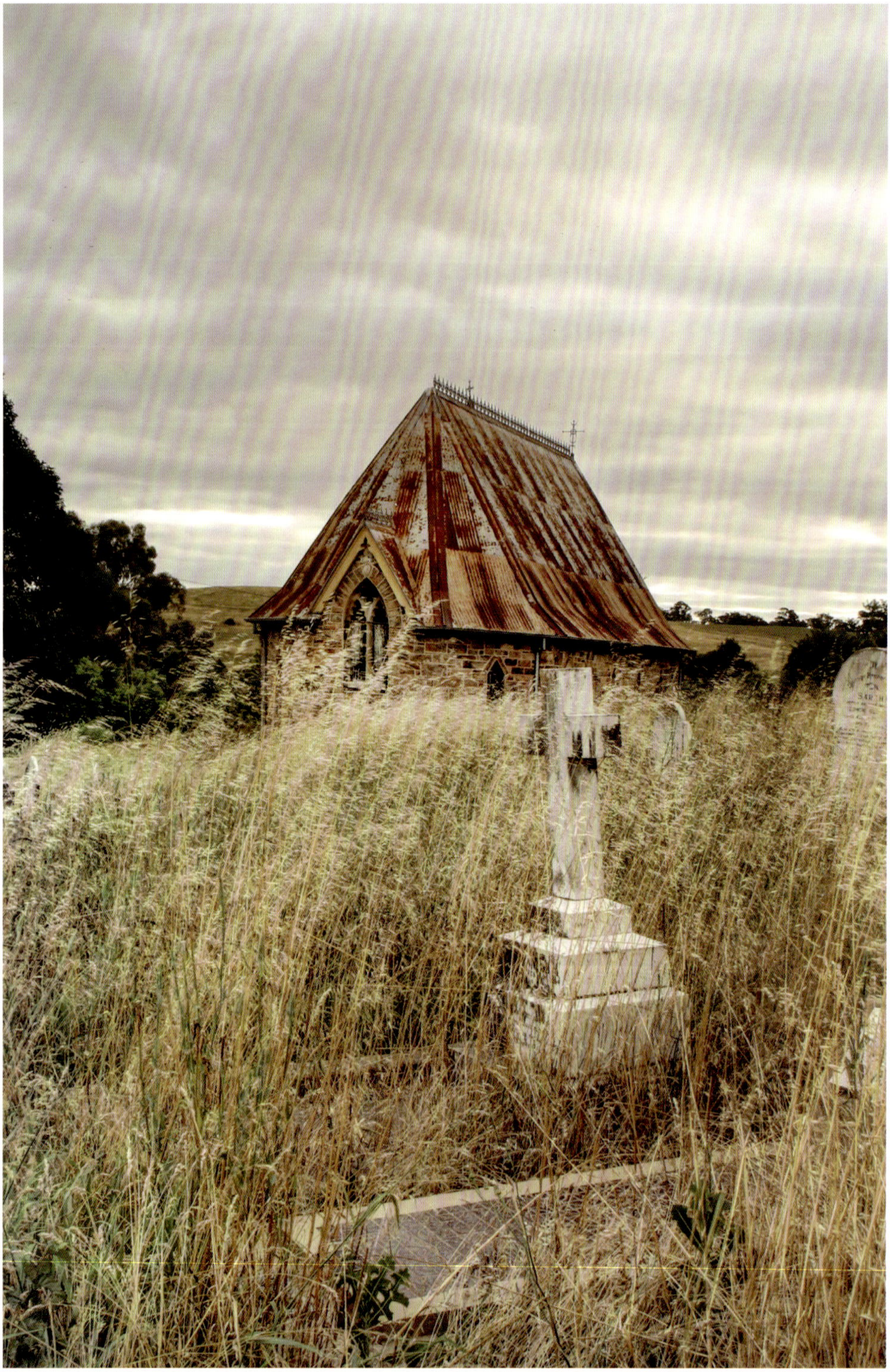

Almost buried in overgrowth, this forgotten chapel sleeps in a tiny mid-NSW township

CHAPELS

New South Wales' abandoned chapels are the religious footprints left behind by dissolving congregations in dwindling towns. Used initially as the village centrepiece for people to meet and worship, a change in demographics combined with society growing slowly more irreligious has left a series of discarded chapels in its wake.

Littered with dirt, bird faeces and feathers, these cobweb-filled relics usually contain very little, although occasionally, the explorer will stumble upon a pew or perhaps a dust-laden bible.

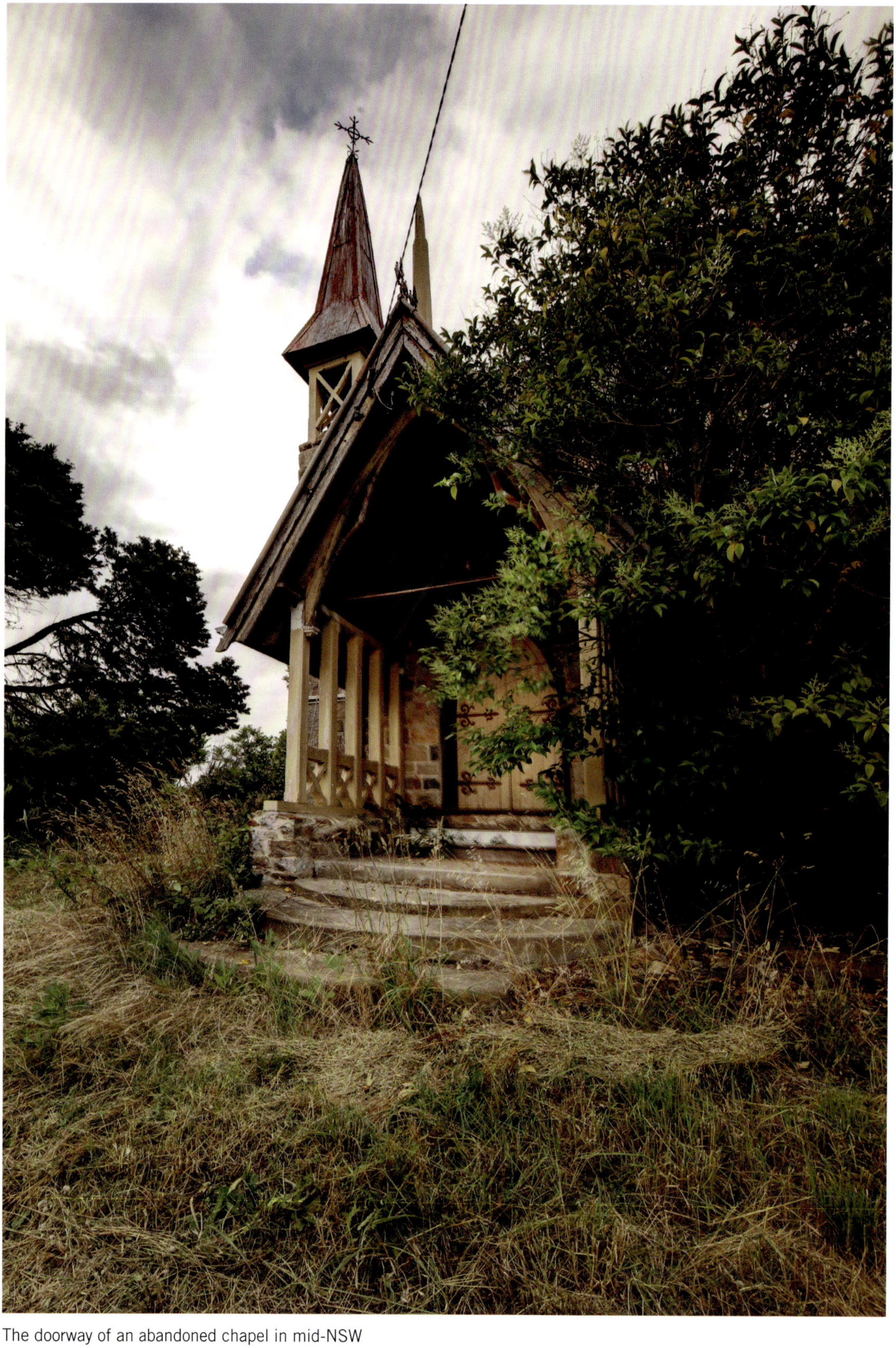

The doorway of an abandoned chapel in mid-NSW

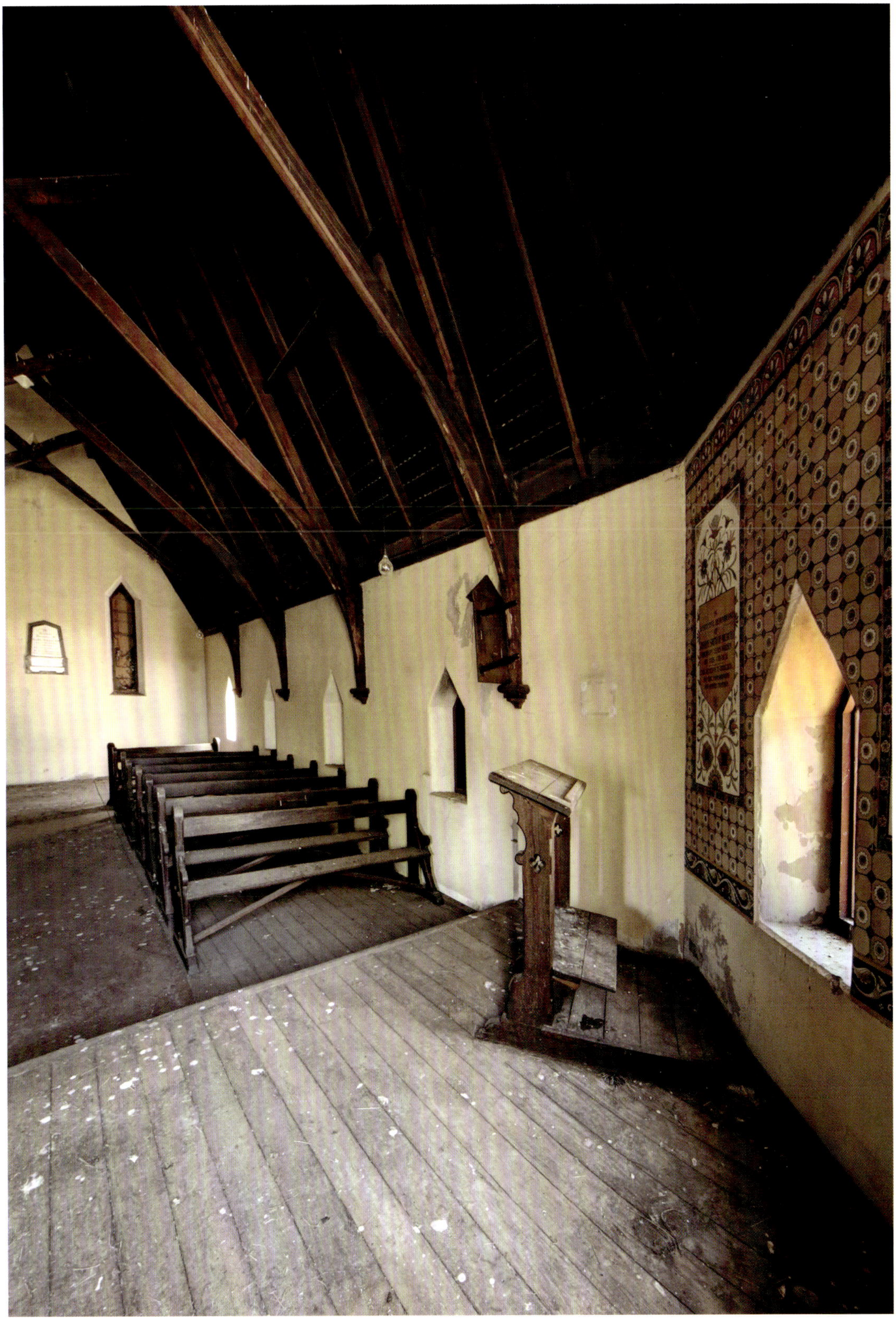

This chapel still contained pews and a wooden pulpit; its interior featured an open truss ceiling and intricately patterned tiling on its front wall

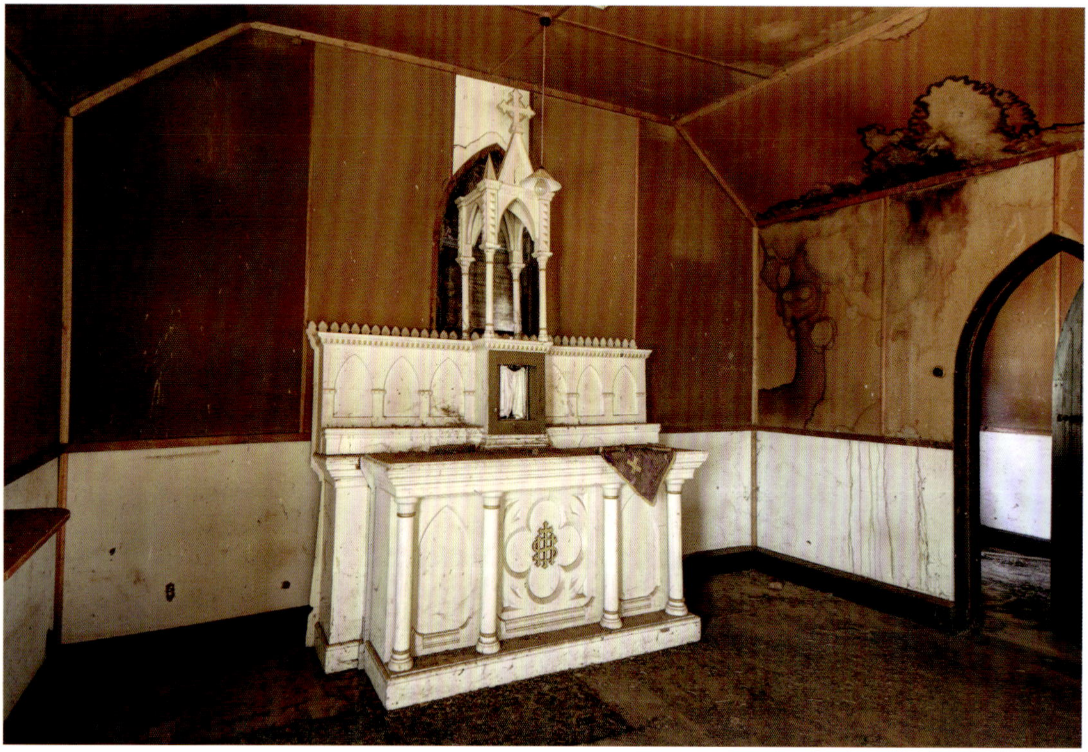

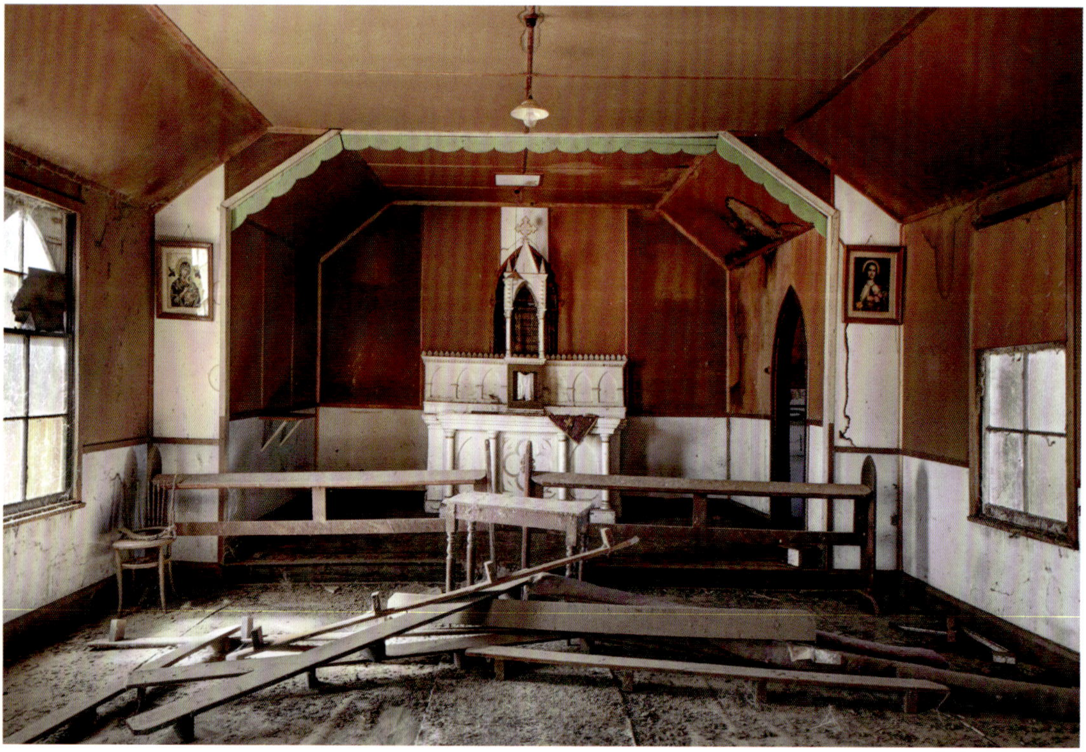

An altar and an array of scattered pews in a long-abandoned country chapel in central NSW

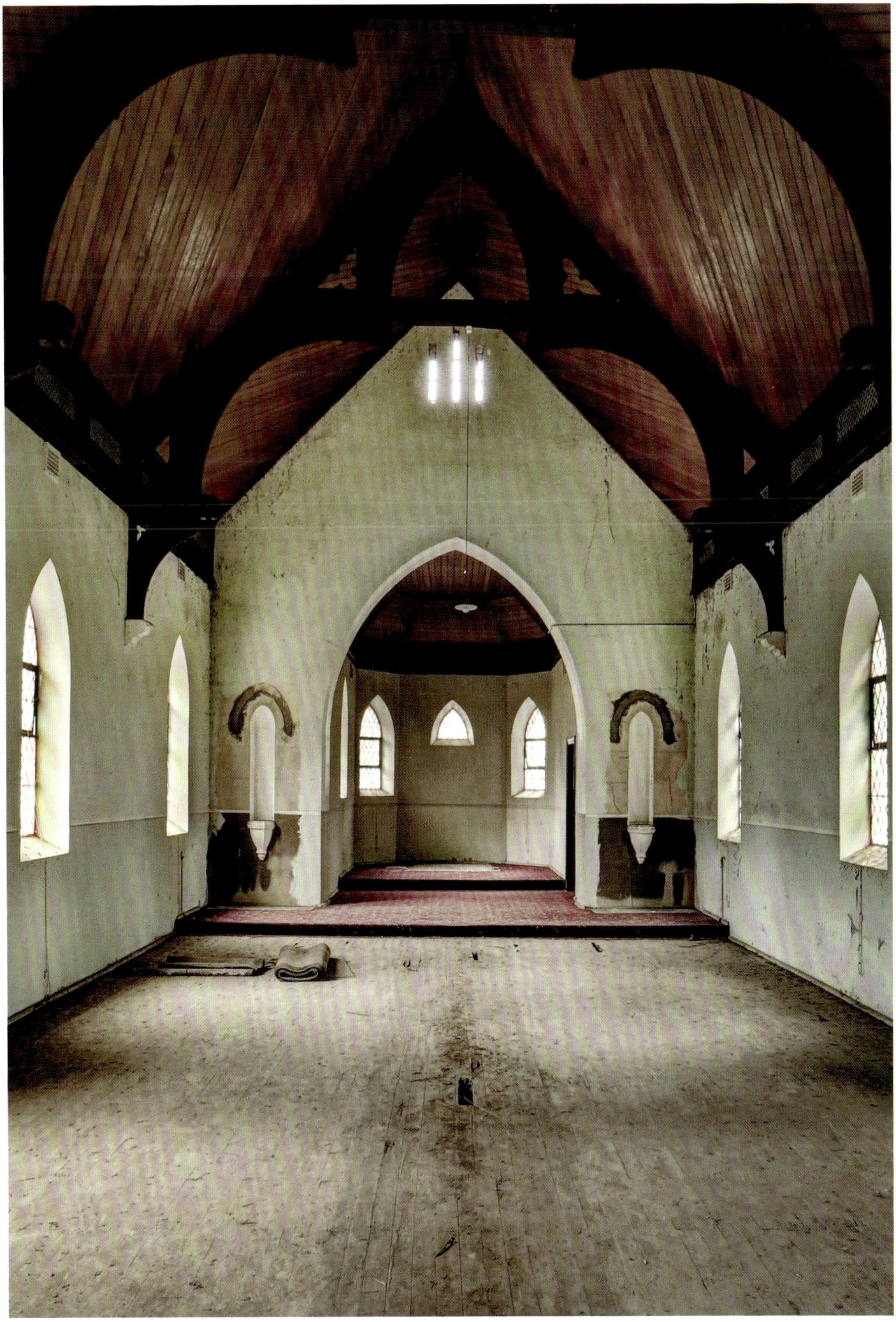

A long view of an abandoned church in central NSW. Its pews and alter have long since been removed.

ALSO FROM WOODSLANE PRESS

The *Australia Through Time* books are published by Woodslane Press. The imprint is best known for Australia's bestselling series of walking guides, available via www.woodslanepress.com.au. If your local bookshop does not have stock of a Woodslane Press book, they can easily order it for you. In case of difficulty please contact our customer service team on 02 8445 2300 or info@woodslane.com.au.

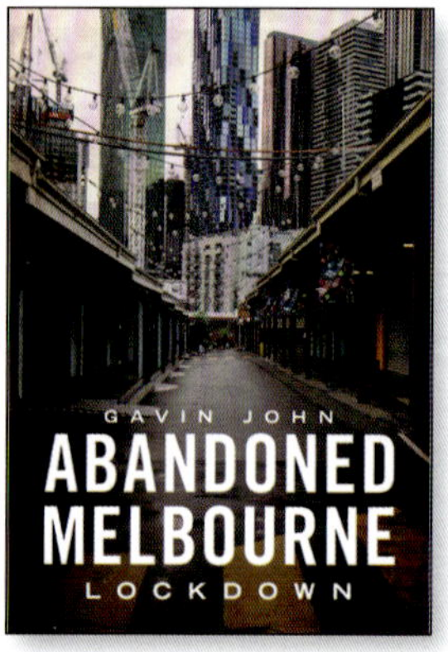

Abandoned Melbourne
$24.99
ISBN: 9781925868715

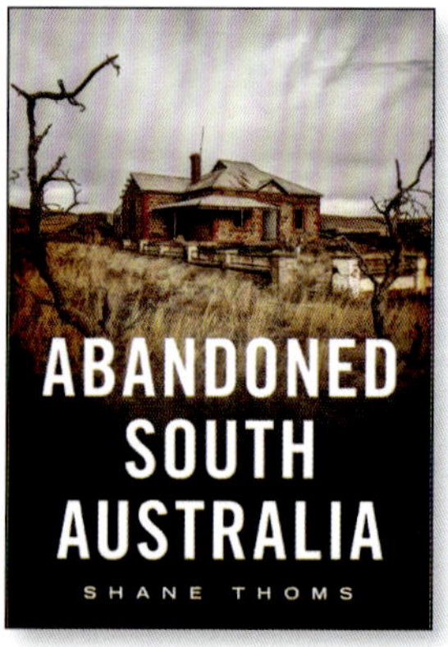

Abandoned South Australia
$24.99
ISBN: 9781925868913

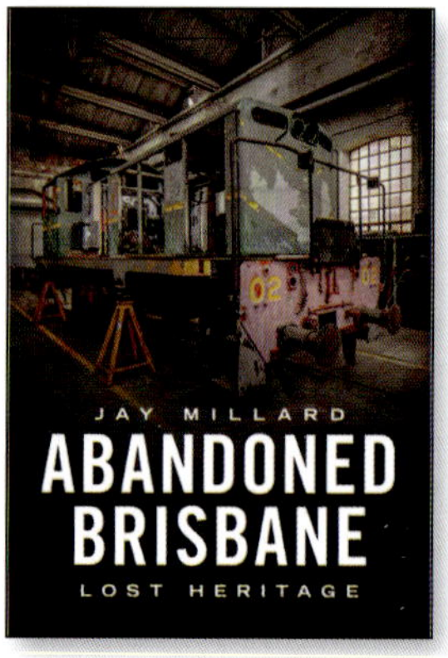

Abandoned Brisbane
$24.99
ISBN: 9781925868722

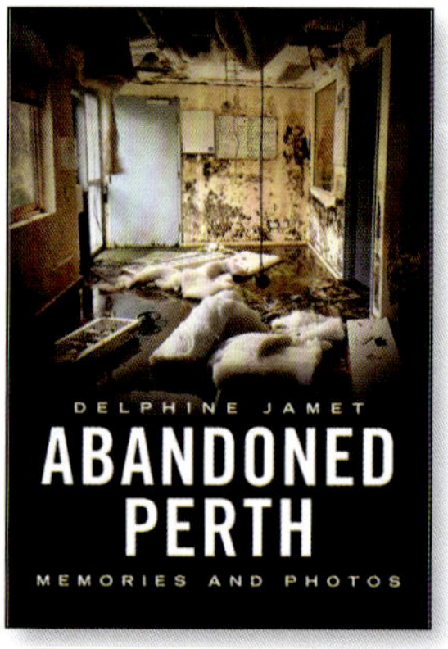

Abandoned Perth
$24.99
ISBN: 9781925868739

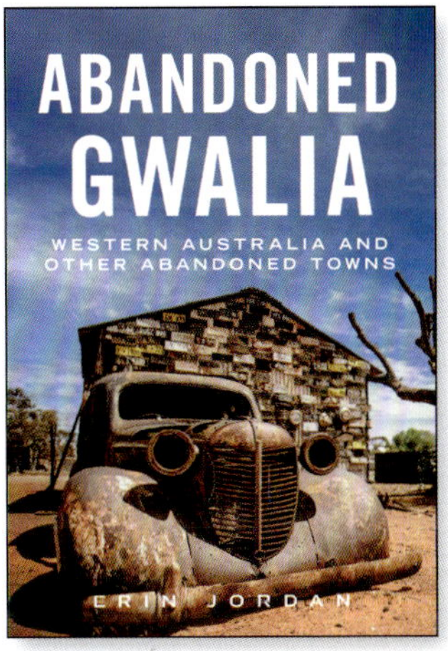

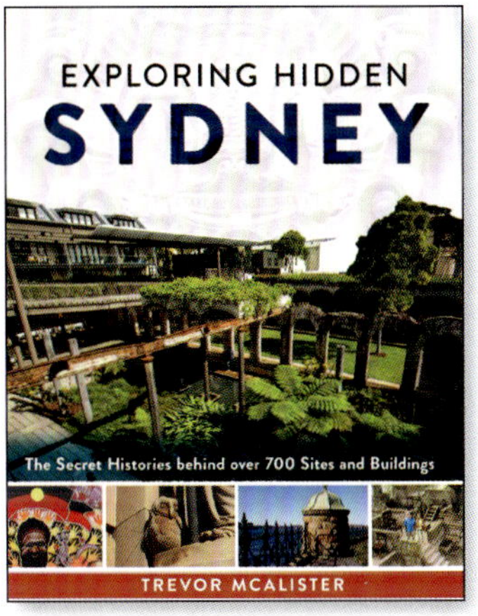

Abandoned Gwalia
$24.99
ISBN: 9781925868906

Exploring Hidden
Sydney
$34.99
ISBN: 9781922800022

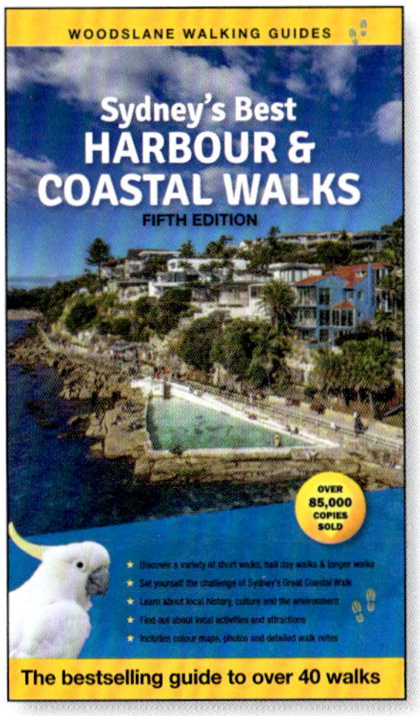

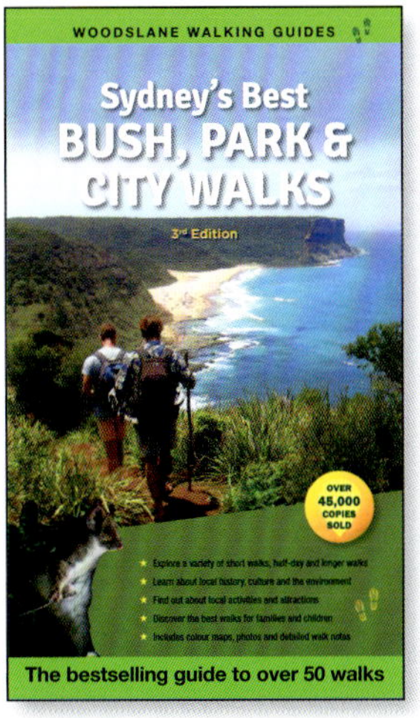

Sydney's Best Harbour
& Coastal Walks
$32.99
ISBN: 9781925868623

Sydney's Best Bush,
Park & City Walks
$32.99
ISBN: 9781925403572

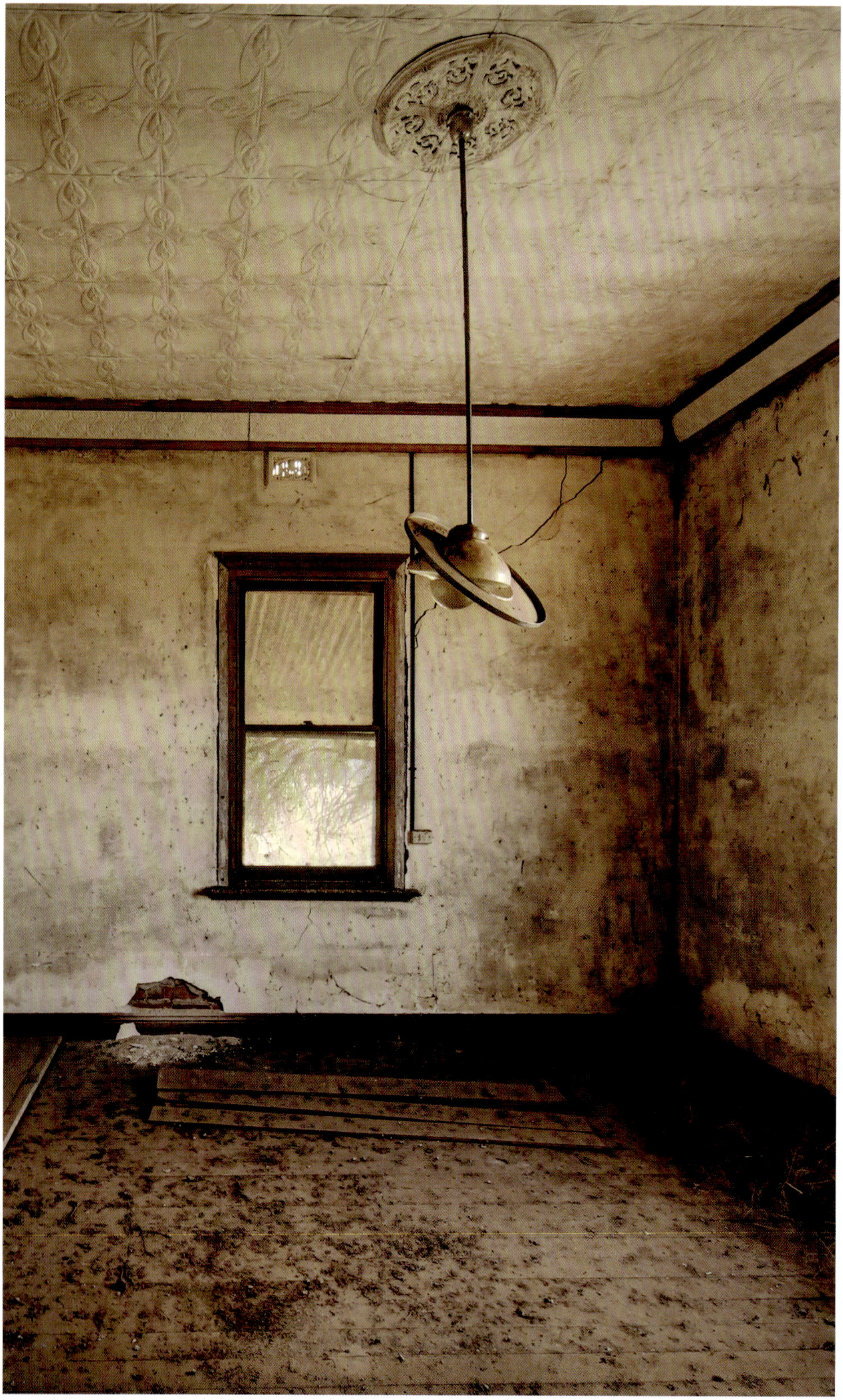